# Selfless

# Selfless

## THE SOCIAL CREATION OF "YOU"

Brian Lowery, PhD

**HARPER**

*An Imprint of* HarperCollins*Publishers*

HarperCollins books may be purchased for educational, business, or sales promotional use. For information, please email the Special Markets Department at SPsales@harpercollins.com.

FIRST EDITION

*Designed by Nancy Singer*

Library of Congress Cataloging-in-Publication Data has been applied for.

ISBN 978-0-06-291300-5

23 24 25 26 27  LBC  5 4 3 2 1

for Cynthia

# Contents

# You'll Be My Mirror

Right now, as I search for the words to express my thoughts to you, I alternate between feelings of frustration and ease. I am certain my self—not you, not anyone else—is having this experience. And you are having your own experience as you read these words. I feel completely whole, able to move through the world and interact with others, or not, as I see fit. I assume you feel the same way: you know that you are *you*, a bundle of experiences, wants and needs, actions taken and avoided, all made coherent because they flow from a single source: *you*.

As we go about our days almost nothing feels as immediate, as wholly our own, as our selves. You are always in there somewhere, thinking and feeling, directing action, like a little "you" managing the controls. But when we take a closer look at the idea of the self as a person inside us, cracks start to emerge.

I have studied social psychology for the past twenty-five years, and I can tell you that our felt experience of the world doesn't always align with what the research shows us. Imagine you won the lottery and all your financial problems vanished.

You can suddenly pay for everything you need and buy just about anything you want. Wouldn't that be fantastic?! Research suggests it probably wouldn't be as good as you imagine. We're actually not very good at predicting the way we will feel in new situations. We tend to overestimate in both directions: we think terrible things will feel worse than they turn out to and expect good things to feel better than they do. We have theories, ideas about ourselves in the world—some accurate, others less so. What we don't have is *direct* access to the way we actually work.[1,2,3,4]

Think of it this way: when we engage with the world, we do so in a way that makes sense to us without needing to understand the incredibly complex processes taking place inside us or the equally complex interactions between us and the external world. It's like the little icons on a computer, our user interface if you will. When you put an item in the "trash," the little icon isn't moving into a trash can. Highlighting something and dragging it to the trash is just a representation of a much more complex set of processes. We engage with the social world in much the same way.[5]

So, when you think, "I love my partner," it's an interpretation of feelings—physical signals from complex biological processes—based on the way relationships work in your culture and your personal history. You've learned what love means and looks like in your culture. Your personal experiences have taught you, among other things, to be guarded or free with your emotions, which affects your willingness to label an experience of someone as love. You can name some of these cultural and personal influences, but others you don't understand or even have access to. Who is to say what past experiences, large or small, were necessary to love our partners? Who knows if in another time or place we would have loved the same person? None of this makes the love we feel right now less real or important; it simply highlights how deeply enmeshed we are in our social world, and how much it affects who we are.

It's obviously not just who we love. What we think of as right or wrong, for example, is also deeply affected by the social world we inhabit. Should children be allowed to play away from their home without supervision? At what age is marriage appropriate? Under what circumstances, if any, is it okay to kill another human being? Answers to these questions have differed across time and continue to differ across cultures and communities.

If you read any of the wildly popular self-help books out there, you might get the impression that we should not want to be shaped by our social environments. Many of these books focus on helping you be unapologetically, unreservedly, your true self. This book doesn't argue against this aim so much as argue that it's not possible. People want and need social engagement, which means we can't live completely free of external influences and constraints.

Much of what we *want* to think about our selves doesn't match reality. Many of us think we are smarter, better looking, and nicer than we really are. When we do good things, like donate money to a charity, we think it's because we're good people. When we do bad things, ignore people in need, we think it's because of circumstances beyond our control.[6] We also have a sense of knowing more than we do about our own psychology. For example, our beliefs about the world often shift, sometimes in ways we don't understand, in response to the beliefs of others. In other words, we are constantly getting things wrong about the way we work. But this is not a book about all the ways we mess up or are messed up. Rather I want to focus on our sense of what we are, what it means to have and be a self.[7,8,9]

Our self is a construction of relationships and interactions, constrained and yet in search of the feeling of freedom. This tension, the need to exist in a coherent way and the desire to do and be whatever we want at any time, defines much of what it means to be human. Where do our experiences of self come from, why do we need the feeling of freedom, why is there a tension between self and freedom, and why does any of this matter?

Our experience of the self must come from somewhere. Our interpretation of our decisions—the story we tell ourselves about who we are—must come from somewhere, and we've looked in a lot of places. Early on, Sigmund Freud theorized that the self was closely tied to sexual development. In the early 1900s, American sociologist Charles Cooley asserted that a person's self, at least in part, is constructed by how they think other people see them—he coined the term "the looking glass self."[10] In the 1930s, sociologist George Mead claimed that the self is developed through social interaction. If you couldn't see yourself through the eyes of others, Mead would say you have no self.[11] Of course, the idea of the self isn't just scientific. Cultural movements have claimed that the self is innate—you're born a certain way and you will not change. Or that your self is handed down from above—God created you. Some Calvinists, for example, believed that people were born predestined for eternal life or damnation.

When you see me what do you see? A man? A Black guy? A professor? Someone in a hoodie? A threat to you, or a new friend?

The truth is, if we meet and interact, you don't just see me. You see what your relationships have taught you about people like me. If you're a native of the United States, we see our shared racial history through the lens of current social concerns like the Black Lives Matter movement. We see each other's gender through recent shifts in gender expectations—maybe we even state our pronouns. You might see me as a professor and engage me around your beliefs about professors' political views. Do you feel comfortable with me, or do you worry I am judging you? Do you assume we're peers or that I am higher or lower status than you? Do you assume we agree on important issues? Do you enter the interaction expecting us to be friends? What you believe about me affects the way you interact with me; your beliefs and actions, in turn, affect the nature of my self. Whether I accept or reject your view of me, it will change me. We bring multifaceted selves to our interactions, and in these interactions co-create each other again and again.

Selves don't emanate from some ineffable light within people. Instead, selves are created in relationships. In every interaction, others—your partner or a friend, a neighbor or a stranger, a delivery person or a police officer—offer up their view of your self. They may not directly say "This is how I see you," but they show you in the way they treat you, the way they speak to you, and even in subtle body language. In every interaction people say something about who they think you are. Do they smile, do they seem fearful, are they rude or respectful? Every interaction offers you a chance to "see" your self. In fact, the *only* way to see your self is through social interactions.

What people reflect back to you isn't some "true" representation of what or who you are, nor of what they are. It's a construction filtered through the self of the person you're inter-acting with. As is their self, in that moment, co-created by you. In the hall of mirrors, we see our selves reflected, or perhaps refracted, in the multitude of people who surround us.

This leads to an important question. When you wonder whether what you say or do is best for your self, you must ask: *Which* self? This might sound like something out of a psycho-logical thriller, wherein one person is both sweet and murder-ous. Dr. Jekyll and Mr. Hyde—one body, but two (or more) distinct selves. Turns out a version of this plot device, though a much less sensational version, is true for all of us.

We all have multiple selves (parent, child, employee, ath-lete, lover, etc.).[12,13] And each of these selves is defined in a web of relationships and has particular attributes. What determines which one we are in any given situation? The biggest determi-nant of who you are is probably *where* you are. And by "where you are" I mean all the features of your situation: physical lo-cation (restaurant versus home), company you're with (friends versus family), nation you're in, and even the time of day. You are a different self at drinks with college friends than at drinks with family after dinner. Think of the last time you were out with close friends. Think about the way you spoke, the language you used, how loudly you spoke. Think about what a stranger looking at you might have thought. Now think about the last time you were in a professional setting, maybe an office meet-ing. Almost certainly you behaved differently. At least I hope you did. You might think you were the same self, but is that really true? Did you feel the same way? Probably not. Both of these "selves" are you, but consider the possibility that they are different *you*s.

Here is the kicker, which probably won't come as a surprise: the contents of our identities are sometimes in conflict. In the United States what comes to mind when you imagine a professor does not align with mainstream social depictions of Black people. When I first walk into a classroom people don't always assume I am the professor. I also have to reconcile my identity as a Black man with my identity as a professor, because I have to manage the relationships that constitute these identities. I am keenly aware that my social status as a professor at a prestigious university is higher than my status as a Black man. Should I display my status as a professor to counteract the social costs of being a Black man? Claude Steele, an eminent social psychologist, tells the story of a young Black graduate student whistling Vivaldi while walking at night in White neighborhoods to assure White people that he is not what they consider a "regular" Black man.[14] But if I "whistle Vivaldi," am I in that moment trying to deny being Black, and in doing so, am I betraying what it means to be a member of the Black community?

To see how people manage conflicting identities, social psychologist Margaret Shih designed a study that examined Asian-American women's relationship to math. As Asian Americans they are stereotyped as *more* proficient at math, but as women they are stereotyped as *less* proficient at math. To study this, Shih and her colleagues asked a group of Asian-American women to self-identify differently: sometimes as Asian American, other times as women. And then they gave them a math test.[15,16,17]

When asked to provide their ethnicity before the test, the participants in the study performed better than those asked to identify their gender. All that had changed was a shift of the mirrors around them, a shift in their reflections. And yet, real outcomes shifted.

This underperformance is most often attributed to the cost of knowing that people expect you to underperform. But that *is* a change in self: the anxiety that affects performance is tied to a change in relationships that define the self. When people thought about themselves as Asian American or as women, their relationships with others shifted and their test performance changed—a tangible result. And that is a *literal* change in their selves.

The self *is* what others reflect back to us. Think about your life. As you navigate the terrain of your social world, how often do the mirrors that constitute your self shift or tilt? One moment you're a parent, then an employee, next a friend. Each of these selves has a bundle of expectations and responsibilities baked in. What tests are you acing or failing because your self has shifted without you even knowing it?

BUT JUST AS THE IDEA of an unchanging self is an illusion, so too is the unfettered freedom that modern society seeks for the self. Being a completely free self isn't possible because without the constraint imposed by relationships you wouldn't have a self at all. You can't be yourself by yourself.

Our understanding of the relationship between self and freedom organizes much of our life and society. There is tension between our desire for autonomy and free will, and the constraints necessary to produce a coherent self in the first place. We sometimes chafe against limits imposed by others, be they friends, lovers, or governments, while seeking out relationships to make life livable and coherent. Who or what would we be without ties to the people and communities that define us? Selfless, perhaps free, but certainly lost.

The idea of being left alone, of being free from external constraint, assumes a clear understanding of the difference between internal and external forces—we feel free when we believe that our thoughts, feelings, and actions are driven by internal forces. The question is what counts as internal. If someone asks to borrow a book from you and you give it to them, was the action free? What if the person who asked to borrow the book only did so to make you feel important? If it worked, but you didn't know that was their intent, was your action driven by internal or external forces? In the first case, you might think you freely lent the book; in the second case you might feel like the person manipulated you. In both cases, you responded to the other person's actions; the difference is your knowledge of their intent. You might say that you don't have the information necessary to act freely if the person misrepresents their intent. But what if the person doesn't fully understand what's driving their behavior? When you drill down, the line between internal and external forces is less clear than it might seem.

Let's explore this distinction between internal and external. Right now, think about the little finger on your right hand. Wiggle it a bit.

We just shared a moment, a little dance across time and space. I had a weird idea, wrote it down, and then you, wherever and whenever you're reading this, acted on it.

There are almost too many moments of magic to count in that little dance. For starters, the incredible complexity of the publishing industry and the many thousands of people necessary to physically make the computer I'm writing this on and the book or device you're reading it on. But here, what matters most to me is that *my* thoughts affected *your* behavior. What does that say about your self? Was your self, the one reading this book, truly separate from mine? Were you free in spite of my presence? Was I—alone, writing at my desk months or years before you read the words I wrote—truly free while imagining you? Or was I constrained by my imagination of you. I don't know you, but I imagine you as a smart, curious, critical reader, and this version of you—in our interaction right now—demands something of me, and thus shapes me at this moment. The idea of you has affected my behavior and what I chose to share in this book, long before you read it. I've read books with you in mind. I've even read this book out loud to see how you might hear it. You have, in other words, made me a writer!

This is to say that the way we define our selves, the separation between you and me, is entwined with the way we think about freedom. I have affected your actions and thoughts, and you've also affected mine, even though we have probably never met.

When you wiggled your little finger, or just thought about doing so, was it my thought or yours that created the action? Did I do something to you? Or did your action bring my thought to life?

Obviously, both are true. If you wiggled your finger, you chose to do so; I couldn't force you to do it. At the same time, you almost certainly wouldn't have done so if I didn't suggest it. And even if you didn't wiggle your finger, you thought about it. You really couldn't have read the sentence and not considered it. If you didn't do it, you *chose* not to. So even though I didn't compel your action, I did compel a decision. What does that say about *my* relationship to *your* self? If you think of your self as, in part, the decisions you make, I just shaped your self. If you think of freedom as freedom from others' influence, I just hampered your freedom. This tiny little interaction between us is a microcosm of your day-to-day life.

Think about your typical day. If you're like me, your day revolves around other people. If you live with other people, soon after you wake up you're navigating relationships: sharing the bathroom; eating with partners, children, or roommates; answering emails and messages from friends or colleagues. You also interact with people you will never meet: maybe you're reading the news about people in some far-off place, the goings-on of celebrities, the announcements of elected officials. All these interactions can take place before we even leave the house for the day.

Now consider the countless encounters, both planned and completely incidental, that occur throughout your day. All these interactions demand something of you; more importantly, they *affect* you. Of course, most of the people you walk past barely register, but that doesn't mean these fleeting interactions have no consequence: even one person seeing you as attractive or unkempt, a threat or a friend, can transform everything you think and do that day. Imagine that your partner or roommate questions the way you're dressed just before you leave the house. Maybe their comment undermines your confidence. You start to worry about the way others will see you. At work you feel less confident giving that big presentation, and it doesn't go as well as it could have. You feel a little less extroverted than normal after work. Maybe you're not as talkative around strangers you bump into. You come home and you're in a bad mood and maybe have a fight with your roommate or partner. This can sound like just a bad day, but these effects reverberate. Maybe you like your job a little less after that lackluster presentation and feel less tied to your professional identity. Or maybe your bad day intersects with your partner's insecurity and a resulting fight forever changes the way you see and interact with each other. Small causes can create big effects.

The behaviors of others affect the way you, in turn, behave in the world. Even when you were reading a book "all by yourself," suddenly a choice was forced upon you by someone you couldn't even see. What other choices are you being forced to make, and by whom?

Society is an intricate social game.[18] We depend on others following rules we understand, and responding, often without thought, to what we are doing. Even if we can't describe the rules, they shape the way we behave. If you ride public transportation, you probably know you don't sit next to someone if an open seat is available farther away. At least in the cities I know, you also don't talk to strangers and generally try to mind your own business. These unspoken rules help minimize uncomfortable situations and disruptions of our daily commutes. The order they provide makes the ride a little easier to tolerate, saves us energy for the day ahead, or allows us to ease into our evenings.

To make it through our days, we need the world to have order. We also need to believe that what we do affects the world, and that the outcomes of our behaviors are, at least in theory, predictable. Imagine you are trying to lose weight. You're doing everything you're supposed to—eating less and exercising more—but you aren't losing weight. It probably wouldn't take too long before you give up. Imagine the same thing for any other area of life, for example your finances—you work and work, but rising prices mean you can't gain any ground. It would be really tough to believe that nothing I do matters, and only a little easier to accept that I can't predict how what I do will affect me or other people. The order we perceive or construct is necessary for the feeling that our choices matter, that we can in fact choose outcomes.[19,20,21]

My goal isn't to push an argument about your ability to decide, but to have you ponder the possibility that the boundary between your and others' selves might not be as clear-cut as it seems. What does it mean, to you, if your self is not what you thought? What does it mean, to you, that the way you engage with others remakes them and affects their relationships? Maybe it would reshape the way we define "our" communities. They might become more expansive, more diverse, more vibrant. Maybe we would take our interactions more seriously. Maybe we would take more responsibility for the state of our relationships and communities.

WITH A BETTER UNDERSTANDING OF self and freedom in hand, we can turn to a different question. What function does self serve? Why do we even need self? Today we just assume the existence of an individual, self-contained, autonomous self, but why? Do we need this idea to function as a community? We need self, at least in part, because unfiltered reality overwhelms us. Self provides order that helps us function. Self is a point of view. Self helps us manage a world that exceeds what we can imagine. Self is a social structure that allows you access to the ultimately unfathomable, blooming, buzzing chaos of reality. A well-functioning self provides a sense of predictability, stability, and certainty.

We immediately understand people and social situations based on often inarticulable cultural and personal information. For example, when someone enters your personal space you feel uncomfortable, but what constitutes too close depends on things like your relationship with the person and where you're from. No one told you how far away strangers or friends or family should stand from you, but nevertheless you know. You probably don't experience it as "that person is standing too close for a stranger in Norway" or Spain or wherever. It's just the feeling that someone is inappropriately close to you. Where did that feeling come from? As I'm sure you know, personal space differs based on your culture. The existence of personal space is universal, but our community determines the way this universal need is experienced. It's the product of unspoken rules you picked up from those around you. The influence of our community is profound, whether we can articulate it or not.

Research finds that humans recognize nonverbal "emotional expressions" regardless of where someone is from. If you're from Germany, you still know what fear looks like in someone from Ecuador. But it turns out that there are community accents in emotional expressions. In one clever study, researchers from Harvard University displayed pictures of either Japanese or Japanese-American people showing either neutral or emotional (fear, disgust, sadness, surprise) facial expressions. Importantly, the photos were designed to eliminate cultural differences in appearance, so for example, the clothing on each subject didn't give hints as to their nationality. Nevertheless, people were significantly better than chance at telling the difference between a Japanese person and a Japanese-American person, and they were significantly better at telling the difference when the person was expressing emotion. In other words, people can identify incredibly subtle, community-created differences in the way people express emotion. We can recognize members of our communities because we know what the influence of the community looks like. Things as personal as your expression of fear and sadness bear the mark of those who define you.[22]

This is all to say that your self is constructed and reconstructed in a swirl of ever-evolving relationships. The ideas that live in these relationships and interactions provide the social identities—for example, gender, ethnicity, professional identity—that we use to make sense of ourselves and others. This self situates you in the world, it provides a perspective, a vantage point, from which you experience the world. The construction of self might be complex, but the experience is pretty straightforward. But there are no free lunches. The simplification that a self provides comes at a cost.

THE FIRST PART OF THIS book explores ideas of self. What exactly is this thing that we feel we know intimately, but in some ways not at all? How does self reveal the truth about our misconceptions of freedom, and much else? Here we will dip into many streams to piece together a view of self. We will also identify weaknesses in what often passes as an obvious answer to this complex question—the idea of self as ineffable soul or biological fate. Instead, I will showcase self as a hall of funhouse mirrors and demonstrate how difficult it is to find freedom within their countless reflections.

In the second part of the book, we will take on the self as a collective idea and explore the way this idea depends on the basic need for human connection, but also challenges the desire for freedom. I argue that the push and pull between the linked desires for structure and freedom, predictability and uncertainty, order and chaos is the human condition that drives much of the social world. And we'll examine this tension between self and freedom within questions of social group identities like race, gender, and nationhood. We will also explore the role of technology in expanding and constraining the self.

In the third part of the book, we explore the implications of the tension between structure and freedom for some of life's biggest questions. To function effectively, we need the world to make sense. Humans need structure, perceived order. But to feel alive, we need the experience of freedom. Imagine tomorrow you woke up and believed that all you have been, are, and will be is fated. Life would lose much of its meaning. The belief that you make decisions freely, and that *your* decisions matter, gives life flavor.

To look out and accept the yawning unknown at our feet is one thing, but to turn our gaze and face the same vast unknown of our selves is something else entirely. It can be deeply uncomfortable to face the possibility that we are not what we think we are. This desire for assurance about who we are can work counter to self-discovery. For example, sometimes we prefer to be around people who bolster the way we already see ourselves, even when we don't like what we see—better the devil we know than have to confront a reflection of ourselves we don't recognize.[23,24] To learn something new about the self requires that we accept there may be challenges to what we believe we know.

More than a few shelves are weighed down with books designed to remind you just how special you are. These books tell you how to find yourself, how to shrug off haters, how to design the life you deserve, how to be your unencumbered, unstifled, authentic, true self—and how knowing yourself is the first step in getting what you want and need. How *you* can be the best *you*. These books speak to those yearning for a certain kind of life, one of happiness, or at least contentment.

This is not one of those books. I won't pander to what we *want* to believe about ourselves: that there is someone in there, inside you, waiting to be set free, to live the life of your dreams. Or that we are, or can be, in complete control of our lives or even know our selves deeply and truly.

We live our lives in complex relation to people and systems. Your parents, siblings, friends, and romantic partners affect who you were, are, and can be. The way we operate within society's institutions limits what we can do, and what you can conceive of. Daydreams of who you can be, what your life might be, or have been, are limited by the cultural materials you have to work with. We can only create from what's available to us.

You are the product of the social world you inhabit. As such, there is no simple formula, no paint-by-numbers route to "fixing" your life. To change your circumstance—to take care of your self—is a *collective* effort. Others create us and we create them. If we want to understand our selves, we must first understand this give-and-take.

# PART I

# You

*and*

# Your

# Self

# 1

## The Search for Self

*I want to tear down the exceptional preeminence now generally awarded to the self.*

—"The Nothingness of Personality," Jorge Luis Borges[1]

When you're driving a car and come to a four-way stop, you assume others will obey the rules of the road as well, and you will all appropriately take turns advancing or turning through the intersection. Each time this happens, it strengthens an unstated faith in the way things work, which increases the chance that you will continue to drive in a way that others find sane and predictable. Now imagine that tomorrow you stop at a corner you know well but others ignore the rules of the road, they drive too fast, run stop signs, turn across multiple lanes of traffic. The same thing happens the next day, and the next.

Now, rather than counting on everyone to follow rules you understand, you have to drive as if anyone might do anything. It probably won't take long for you to ignore rules you have followed for years. You can't assume others will stop at a red light, so you might have to slow down and maybe even stop at a green light just to make sure someone doesn't crash into you. For driving to continue without utter chaos, new rules would have to emerge, and you would learn, very quickly, to adopt them.

Let's take another example—a *Freaky Friday*–esque thought experiment. Let's say you switch bodies with someone quite different from you and are accordingly treated as they are typically treated; the old rules you had learned to abide by would eventually cease to apply. Now, when you speak, people pay either more or less attention than they did before. Where before, when you walked into a store, you garnered positive (or negative) attention, now the reverse is true. People who previously ignored you now speak to you, and people who spoke to you now ignore you. It's like everyone ignoring stop signs when the day before they mostly obeyed the rules of the road. When such things happen to you now, you notice them as anomalies to be explained. Something just feels off even if you can't put your finger on it. But if this became your new normal—if the old social structure shimmered, shifted, and fell away—you would become a new self.

This actually happens to us throughout our lives, though much more gradually than in a sci-fi body-switching situation. The rules you have as a child—early bedtime, no crossing the street alone, eat your vegetables—shift and change as you grow into a teenager. Where once you weren't allowed to venture too far from home without supervision, you now might roam many miles from home without your parents knowing exactly where you are. Such changes happen again when you become an adult, and yet again when people start to see you as elderly. In fact, the very elderly often end up with roles similar to the ones they had as children: they're watched more carefully, lose some control over their independence, like driving and banking, and sometimes even need someone to feed them. Although you'll never actually switch bodies with someone else, you do become a new self, many new selves, over the course of your life.

There is a game you can play with cards to demonstrate how you come to understand your self through others. Maybe you've played it. Each person in the group is given a playing card, which assigns them a "value," and is told to hold it against their forehead for everyone but themselves to see. People are told to interact with each other as if each person *is* the value of their card. If you encounter someone with a King card you would interact with them as if they are someone worthy of great respect, or at least deference. If you encounter someone with a Three card, you might think of them as janitors or cashiers, jobs that don't earn a lot of money or societal respect. How you treat each person is indicative of how you perceive them socially. At the end of some amount of time, everyone is asked to guess their own card. Most times I've seen this game, people's guesses are surprisingly accurate. Without ever seeing their own card, they can usually guess their position within a card or two. This is a simple version of the game we all play every day. We understand our selves based on the rules provided by our culture and the way we are treated.

We all know our self intimately, but only vaguely understand it. Sometimes when surprised by our behavior, or where we find ourselves in life, we might ask, *Who am I? How did I get here? How did this become my life?* But in each of these questions, there is an unstated assumption that we at least know what—who—that "I" is.

Selves are mysterious. We cannot escape our self—no matter what you do or where you go, you are with your self. Given all the time we spend with our selves, you would think we would understand them better. But if you're anything like me, you often surprise yourself, sometimes for the better, sometimes for the worse. It's tricky to see the self clearly when we expect the self to be an internal, stable essence.

Think of the self like a nation. The government changes, citizens come and go, but the nation remains more or less the same. The continuity of interactions among people, the belief in a continuous history and national culture creates the experience of a stable entity. The idea of nation is often linked to a physical boundary, a country's borders, but borders don't define nations. A nation is composed of the relationships among people who believe themselves to be members of the nation. A nation is defined by selves. A self is more like a nation composed of interactions among people than it is like a country defined by a physical boundary. Nations and selves are defined by shared understandings within a network of relationships. Self, in other words, *is* a shifting structure of social relationships and interactions.[2]

SELVES ARE PERSPECTIVES FROM WHICH we view others and we assume that these others view us from their perspectives. For this to work we have to interact with others as if they exist in much the same way we do. I can write to you because I assume you will ponder and decide to accept or reject whatever it is I have to say, in much the same way I would. Our connection depends on my assumption that you have a mind similar to my own. In technical terms, I have a theory of mind: I believe your mind exists in much the same way that I believe mine does. I am capable of imagining things as other than they are and of trying to convey this alternate reality to you. And I assume you can do the same.

When, in the Introduction, I asked you to wiggle your little finger, you probably wondered why. This question assumes that I have reasons much like you do. You might also wonder where I plan to lead you, what's going on in my mind, what my goals are, what I'm trying to accomplish. I wrote my little idea hoping it would allow you to understand my thoughts about our relationship a little better. And to illustrate how social interactions and relationships work.

We act, and act on each other. In important life-defining relationships and in fleeting, seemingly inconsequential interactions our choices and actions are shaped by the choices and actions of those around us. Growing up in the 1980s and '90s, I moved around a lot—Mississippi to Chicago to California. In fact, I went to six different schools in Chicago before attending college. My parents made their decisions to move (and move again) for complex reasons, and these decisions affected me and the way I interacted at each new school I attended. I've played the new kid many times over, which taught me how to interact as an outsider. It probably also taught me many other skills that are useful in some situations, but problematic in others. For example, in new situations, even today, I quickly create a tight social circle, which provides me with support and insight into the new setting, but doing so might also be prematurely cutting me off from other useful or satisfying relationships. By shaping my relationships and the way I create them, my parents inadvertently shaped the way I behave. I'm sure you can point to examples when other people's behavior affected who you are or what you've become, for better or worse. Even as an adult, if your partner decides to take a new job or your child plays this sport instead of that one, it affects you. Do you have to move cities for your partner, or drive your kid all over the place for games, meets, or matches? Do you move to an intensely conservative or liberal area? Do you spend time with other "sport parents"? Are you a "trailing" spouse spending lots of time with your partner's work colleagues? Each of these possibilities would affect you in ways that are both obvious and opaque to you.

It's easy to see how the big decisions made with those closest to you, like your partner taking a job in another city, directly affect you. But you're also affected by little incidental interactions all the time. Think about the last time a stranger gave you an unexpected compliment. How did it feel? How might it have affected the way you interacted with someone else later that day? Maybe it brightened your mood. Maybe it made you feel a little more confident. Now imagine how a happier, more confident *you* behaved the rest of your day and interacted with others. Other people's behavior changes the way we feel, what we think, and the way we behave.

But don't our internal characteristics affect the way we feel, think, and behave? Yes. There is evidence that people are born with biological predispositions toward certain characteristics (i.e., temperaments), which affect their response to social situations.[3,4,5] If by temperament I am anger-prone and someone shouts at me, it might provoke a physical altercation. If I tend to be shy, it might elicit tears. But features of the situation matter, too. The size and perceived fighting skill differential between me and my verbal assailant will affect how much I want to fight. It's also the case that my history in similar circumstances—have I had physical fights before?—will affect my behavior. Yet, no matter what, the behavior of the other person, as well as my beliefs about why they behaved as they did, will affect my response.

The idea that the self is so dynamic might sound ludicrous. You might feel like you *know* it can't be true. It's a funny thing about knowledge that the pure commonplaceness of a thing can create the feeling of understanding it. And there is nothing that we spend more time with than our selves, which might give the feeling of knowing it, but what do we really understand about self?

Consider the 2,500-year-old Oracle of Delphi. Etched above the temple was the phrase "Know Thyself." If moving through life was sufficient to lay bare the self, the exhortation to "Know Thyself" wouldn't make sense: it would be the same as saying "Live." The phrase "Know Thyself" whispers that things aren't what they seem, or at least are vastly more complicated than they appear.

When asked about their "true self," people often point to moral traits, like empathy and generosity, or negative traits like cruelty and selfishness: traits we perceive to distinguish between good and bad people. We tend to think that traits we use to distinguish between right and wrong form the essence of "self." In one study of our perception of others' selves, a group of people were asked to imagine that a person in the near future had suffered a car accident and as a result, had undergone brain replacement surgery. The study participants were told that one of five things happened after the surgery: 1) the person is the same, 2) the person is the same, but can't recognize objects even though they can see perfectly fine, 3) the person has lost all desire, but acts and thinks the same, 4) the person lost all his memories, but acts and thinks the same, 5) the person lost his moral conscience, meaning he can no longer judge right from wrong, but otherwise he acts and thinks the same. It turns out being told a person has lost their moral conscience had the largest effect on the sense that this person is no longer him or her self. In a related study the same researchers found that traits people connect to personality (e.g., shyness, industriousness, and anxiousness) are less strongly correlated to our idea of their "self" than traits that connect to morality (e.g., conscientiousness, politeness, and empathy).[6]

Who am I then? I think of myself as someone committed to justice, someone who cares about equal access to opportunity, who places others' life outcomes above abstract ideas. What could be more "me" than the beliefs I hold most dear? Unlike some careers or even some relationships, you don't fall into your beliefs; you must choose them. And there is nothing stopping you from choosing this or that belief. You don't have to be born with money, go to a particular school, or know anybody special. You don't even have to reveal your beliefs if you don't want to. All you have to do is choose. What could be more self-defining than this?

You know who you are deep down, in your heart of hearts. You know that you mean well, that you only do the wrong thing when you must or when the situation requires it. If you hit someone it was to defend yourself, or to protect someone, or to teach someone a lesson, or because everyone would've taken the liberty if they could. In any case, your view of yourself, or your thoughts and actions as moral (or not), feels defining.

What if this is all bullshit? What if the self isn't something inside you, in your heart or anywhere else? What if the self is created in social interactions, in shared stories? If actions and beliefs define you, it's only because they have *social* meaning. If you give money to a person in need or a cause to help the downtrodden, are you a good person or a sucker? It's not the action per se that defines you, it's how the action is understood by others, and therefore by you. If people whose opinions you value believe that effort and talent alone should—and *do*—determine people's outcomes, you might be a sucker. You're giving money to someone who clearly doesn't deserve it, denying your self enjoyment, and maybe even supporting someone's laziness. On the flip side, if people whose opinions you value believe that people's situations, through no fault of their own, can create hard times, you might be lauded for helping someone down on their luck and feel good about your self for doing so. We make sense of behavior and beliefs in the context of our relationships. If beliefs and actions define you, it's because they exist in relationships that define you.

WE OFTEN BELIEVE WE CAN see reality clearly, that what we experience *is* reality.[7] This creates a challenge for me if I want you to consider my view of self—which I do—and my view doesn't fit your experience of your self; either your experience is not a direct reflection of reality or my view of self is wrong. Here it's important to distinguish between objective reality, the kind of thing that we can verify through experimentation (i.e., empirical science), and subjective reality, our *perception* of reality. If my view *feels* wrong, we are talking about your subjective experience of reality—the way the world appears to you. People are often more concerned with what *feels* real than with what can be proved empirically. This should come as no surprise given the power of conspiracy theories and cults of all types. But it's important to keep in mind that subjective reality does not necessarily reflect objective reality. I am asking that you consider the possibility that you don't exist in the way many of us feel we do, that there is no internal, stable, unchanging core you were born with that captures your self. I am asking that you consider the possibility that your self is a flux of interactions and relationships *and* your feeling of your self is created in that same flux.[8],[9]

I get that this sounds crazy. I have a strong sense of my internal life, too: the feeling that I exist as a singular being, inside my head, sometimes only weakly attached to others. And yet, as a social psychologist, I'm constantly reminded that individuals lack direct internal access to the way their minds work. Experimental psychologists often examine individuals' responses to novel social situations. Here you should understand the term "social situation" very broadly to mean anything that deals with the presence, real or imagined, of other people.[10] By this definition, a social situation is everything from sitting next to a stranger to voting for a politician to paying someone for a service or looking at pictures of friends, family, or strangers.

Few moments in our lives, in fact, aren't social. Going to work, the grocery store, the dog park, watching a movie, or sitting in church pews—all these situations exert more influence on our lives than we realize, which is really saying something because I would guess you recognize that social situations are powerful. It's just that they are more powerful than we know or typically understand.

Recently a colleague and I were talking about the ideas in this book in front of some graduate students. My colleague challenged the idea that the self is fluid. As I often do, I made the most extreme claim possible. I claimed that the self is *completely* fluid, that the self changes from moment to moment, becoming something new with each change. I claimed that I was changing *her* self at that very moment. She was becoming something, someone, new, in every moment. I reminded her that in previous discussions about her work and mine, she had agreed that I was able to change her mind about the way selves work and the way identities function and that this change in the way she thought about the world and her work was a change in her self. She responded that it wasn't as if I changed her from an introvert to an extrovert or changed her from a liberal to a conservative. I agreed but pointed out that while we could argue how much change is necessary to count as a change in self, she couldn't deny there had been some change.

Putting aside whether you would consider my colleague's change of mind in accepting the idea of a fluid self to be a significant change in her self, I want to point out that the exchange also affected the graduate students watching the interaction. They might have learned that I'm opinionated or that my colleague is stubborn. They might have learned that my colleague and I enjoy arguing with each other. In that situation they might have also understood that disagreeing is an appropriate thing for academic colleagues to do, and that, as academics, they should engage in the same way. Maybe some of the students have learned, through other relationships, that they shouldn't argue.

These students might come to think that academia is not the place for them. Even though the students weren't active in the discussion, merely witnessing the conversation influenced their understanding of what it means to be an academic. Social interactions are reflected and refracted through all the selves involved, which produces effects of such complexity that they are very likely beyond prediction.

THESE PROFOUND AND OFTEN IMPERCEPTIBLE effects mean that we don't see reality as it is. We don't take in information through our senses and reconstruct the reality that's out there. The perception of structure is not a dispassionate recognition of truth. Research suggests that our perception of structure is motivated: when faced with uncertainty, a loss of control, or confusion, we seek out structure.[11,12] Our minds *construct* a reality designed to help us navigate the world effectively.[13] Gestalt psychology, born in the early twentieth century, held that the human experience could not be understood more deeply by breaking it down into basic sensory inputs. They provide evidence of this in perception.[14,15]

In many situations, we see structure in unrelated pieces of information. A set of lines that outline a circle is not a circle; still, you will see a circle there. We tend to fill in blanks. This process is called reification, defined as seeing a collection of individual objects as a meaningful whole rather than separate elements. We don't see the world objectively. Our prior knowledge, experiences, and need for structure affect what we experience.

Psychologists in the United Kingdom recently conducted a study in which they showed people a simple animation. Three colorful blocks were lined up so that the first moved, then the second, and then the third. In one case, the first block appears to hit the second, which pushes into the third, causing the third to move. Think of billiard balls hitting each other, or dominoes falling down. In another case, each block moved the same amount and in the same direction, but the order of events was shifted. In this case, the second block couldn't have caused the third to move, because the third one moved first. This sequence of events doesn't match the way we have come to expect the world to work—Newton's first law of motion: an object will not change its motion unless a force acts on it. When the researchers asked people to describe what happened, they reported seeing what would make sense to them—the second block hit the third, causing it to move—even though this wasn't what was presented to them. We don't see the world as it is, we see what makes sense to us. Such examples provide evidence of the perception of coherence where it doesn't exist. Much like a rose is more than soft fragrance and velvet petals. In each of these cases, we don't see discrete elements; we create a whole that makes sense to us, that fits what we believe the world is, or what we need it to be.[16]

These effects aren't limited to perceptions of inanimate objects. To be human is to interact with humans, but humans are a messy lot. It's hard to make sense of what other people are doing. *Why did she say that? When he did that what did it mean? Does this person like me?* Questions and doubts about what people think or why they do what they do pop up in all of our relationships—with family, friends, teachers, bosses, co-workers, and even someone you bump into on the street. We try to figure out what makes people tick, but sometimes people are an incoherent, cacophonous mess of feelings, thoughts, and actions. We seek order and meaning, and so we fill in the broken lines to create it.

To succeed at being human means coming to terms with the complexity of other people. The problem is we have limited time, information, and ability to do this. If we had to figure out each person we encounter, we would be quickly overwhelmed. So, what do we do? We use shortcuts and tricks to cobble together structure we can understand, a meaningful and predictable world.[17]

To make sense of other people we augment limited information with stories. We put people in groups and extend information about some members to all members. When we see a woman pouring coffee before a meeting, we might assume she is a secretary, and our expectations of secretaries allow us to predict her behavior and interact with her according to a shared story. Within some professional settings during some time periods, secretaries might be seen as low-status, workplace servants—people treated nicely (maybe), but not really respected. In this case, you might request coffee or expect her to answer a phone without giving the request or her feelings much thought. Once an acquaintance of mine, a young(ish) Black man, had just finished dinner and was waiting in the front of the restaurant for the valet to bring his car around. A White couple walked out and asked him if he could get their car, assuming he was the valet. If he had been a White man of equivalent polish, it's unlikely they would have made the same error. We make assumptions, based on our limited knowledge, to help us simplify and navigate the social world. These assumptions provide a structure that we can use, but sometimes they lead us astray.[18]

The sort of examples I've just used often cause consternation. Some argue that such stereotypes are useful because of their statistical truth. Fine. My point is that we don't use them because we have some sixth sense for statistical truth—we hold and act on plenty of beliefs that are demonstrably false. We use these stories because they hold our world together. We create structure because we need the world to make sense. We want predictability to create a sense of control. We not only create stories, we cling to them for comfort and security, and when they come under threat, we defend them. Our need for structure is strong. We are sense-seeking and creating creatures.[19,20]

Structure fills an existential need. Structure is a map of the world around us, with a place for us within it. For some, this might come from "God's plan"; for others, the idea of meritocracy, that everyone's outcomes are the product of individual effort and talent, plays a similar function.[21] We can only be who we are if there is a sensible world around us. But not all structure is consciously considered. Perhaps the most important structures are ones we take for granted: you and I. The idea that you exist as a self is the foundation from which we engage with the world. Imagine you didn't feel your self to be a man or woman, to have an ethnicity or a professional identity, that you had no political affiliation. Imagine you saw little or no difference between friends and strangers, and that friends treated you no differently than strangers. Imagine you had no outlook informed by connections with others. Without a sense of self, and a belief that other selves exist in much the same way, the world would be almost impossible to navigate.

Science, religion, and philosophy are also structures that help us understand our place in the world. Scientists create ideas about the way the world works—theories—and use them to generate hypotheses that can be tested against what we observe. Philosophers rely on rational inquiry to explore fundamental truths about our experience and reality itself. Religious adherents attempt to make sense of the world through faith in supernatural forces. Each of these—science, religion, and philosophy—exists as a communal practice. Science has disciplines, religion has faiths, philosophy has schools, communities that through collective action establish and police boundaries, mint new practitioners, and maintain these structures. With just a little bit of distance we can see the role of people in the creation and operation of science, religion, and philosophy. But not so much the self. The self can seem numinous, emanating from some place beyond human creation. But that is far from true.

Structures—including your self—are created and maintained through collective action. A person who lives in a purely personal world is considered insane. Meanwhile, the more people who join you in a collectively created world the saner you seem, regardless of the content of that world. As I write this, there are people who believe that some leaders of the Democratic Party in the United States are a part of a satanic cult that drinks the blood of children. Surprisingly large numbers of people can believe outlandish ideas if they believe them together. The inverse is also true. Not believing the accepted reality of your social group—whatever that entails—marks you as naïve, corrupt, or mentally ill.

IF OUR SELF AND SENSE of reality is a collective construction rather than a reflection of objective reality, maybe it's not so surprising to learn that people often have a hard time predicting their own behavior. We don't have access to an objective view of our selves because an objective view doesn't exist. Asking someone what they think or what they would do in a particular situation is no substitute for putting them in the actual situation and observing what they do. Even after someone has done either this or that, their story for why they did what they did is often wrong. Even if you offer to pay people to get it right, people are still often unable to correctly identify the impetus or goal of their behavior.

How do I know that? Because an experimenter can control features of a situation that produce the behavior. If you've been to a hotel recently, you've probably noticed that they encourage the reuse of towels and sheets instead of automatically offering clean ones every day. One hotel's actual messaging, for example, says "HELP SAVE THE ENVIRONMENT. You can show your respect for nature and help save the environment by reusing your towels during your stay." Researchers correctly identified this program as a prime opportunity to study how persuasion works and how those under its sway report their motivations. In the experiment, the hotel displayed a different version of the message in some rooms: "JOIN YOUR FELLOW GUESTS IN HELPING TO SAVE THE ENVIRONMENT. In a study conducted in Fall 2003, 75% of the guests participated in our new resource savings program by using their towels more than once. You can join your fellow citizens in this program to help save the environment by reusing your towels during your stay." In yet other rooms, the researchers focused on the guests' room number. The message read: "JOIN YOUR FELLOW GUESTS IN HELPING TO SAVE THE ENVIRONMENT. In a study conducted in Fall 2003, 75% of the guests who stayed in this room ### [room number listed] participated in our new resource savings program by using their towels more than once. You can join your fellow guests in this program to help save the environment by reusing your towels during your stay."[22]

What do you think would matter more to you, being a citizen or being a guest of a particular hotel room?

Most people guessed that, had they read those messages during a hotel stay, they would identify more as a citizen than as a guest in a particular room. But when actual guests saw one or the other message, people who saw the message that connected them to previous guests in their rooms were the most likely to reuse towels.

It turns out that people have a hard time identifying what affects their behavior because their theories—like many theories about our selves—are often wrong. The stories we tell about what affects us, what we care about, or what we think we should care about often don't capture what careful observation and controlled studies reveal. You probably wouldn't expect to be much affected by a message about what past guests in your hotel room did. Yet it turns out that such a message is more persuasive than we expect. A shift in the social situation—thinking about the behavior of people similar to us, even when the similarity feels irrelevant—can affect our behavior in ways that we are unlikely to predict. Just like me asking you to wiggle your finger, just like the Asian-American women taking math tests. When the mirrors shift, so do you.

YOU MIGHT THINK THAT WHILE you don't have direct access to the way your mind works—like the way your ethnicity or gender might affect your math performance or why you forget some things and remember others or why you feel sad in one situation but angry in a similar one—you do have access to your sensations. That seems right. You directly experience what red looks like. But, when we think about our internal states, we're rarely thinking about pure sensation. Your experience of a deep red coupled with a warm floral scent, tied to soft petals and sharp thorns, is not the same as your experience of a rose. A rose is a holistic experience of color, scent, and touch. It's the meaning we make of a set of sensory inputs. This meaning evokes a slew of other memories and feelings. A rose is never just a rose. As with a rose, so with love, boredom, or intellectual delight. These labels represent boundaries that give a sense of unity to a complex array of sensations. Discrete sensations are made into a larger, more meaningful whole.

If you believe your experience transcends individual sensations of taste, touch, smell, sight, or sound, you might also believe your self is more than your body. Want more evidence? It's possible to create the feeling that an animate object is part of your body. If a person's vision is manipulated so that a rubber hand seems to be where their hand would be, and then the rubber hand is touched at the same time as the person's real hand, they will develop the partial sense that the rubber hand is part of their body. They will startle if the rubber hand is smashed by a hammer.[23]

In a related and telling effect that psychologists call enfacement, people are shown to connect their selves to another person's face. Researchers create this feeling using something called Interpersonal Multisensory Stimulation, or IMS for short. That's a very fancy way of describing the experience of watching someone have, in this case, their face touched in exactly the same way and at exactly the same time that your face is being touched. Psychologist Anna Sforza and her colleagues tested this phenomenon with fourteen pairs of volunteers, who had similar facial characteristics (e.g., were the same gender and race). While one of the participants wore a rigid white paper funnel around their eyes so they could only see the face of their partner, a trained experimenter touched both people's faces the same way at exactly the same time with identical paintbrushes. Afterward, the person wearing the funnel was shown a series of images, starting with one of their own face followed by photos that increasingly morphed their face into their partner's until the last photo was just their partner's face. Interestingly, people who underwent the simultaneous touch experience tended to misidentify photos that were composed of 51–59 percent of their partner's face as composed of mostly their own face. They literally saw some of their partner's face in their selves![24,25]

In some ways the enfacement effect shouldn't be surprising. We must have some flexibility in the connection between our selves and our bodies to allow for the fact that changes in our bodies do not necessitate changes in our sense of self. As you get older or as moles appear on your face, you have no trouble recognizing the face in the mirror as yours. On the other hand, it might come as a surprise that we can include the face of another in our selves.

THE SELF AS I DESCRIBE it does not exist inside the body. Even so, this self is both affected by, and affects, the body. The body is the physical entity around which a self is formed. And the body affects the social interactions and relationships, based on race, gender, class, and a thousand other social cues, which in turn affect self.

When your body comes into the world its features affect the way others engage with it. It matters if you're male or female, tall or short, if your skin tone is light or dark, whether you are considered attractive or not. These dimensions of difference shape the self because they shape the way people interact with us. For example, research suggests that mothers are more affectionate, playful, and attentive with attractive versus unattractive babies. If a baby is cute, they'll receive more affectionate caregiving and more interactive play than a baby some might consider ugly. This early difference in interaction echoes throughout a person's adult life. In general, people pay more attention to attractive people and attractive people tend to develop better social skills than their less attractive peers.[26,27]

I don't expect anyone to be surprised that physical features of the body affect the creation of the self. But let's go a step further. Our genetic makeup might also affect the way we see, or influence what we pay attention to in our environment. Social rejection, or the fear of social rejection, is a significant source of pain for many of us. Now imagine a body that is less sensitive to stress than an otherwise identical body—perhaps pain is experienced a little less acutely. If someone's body, let's call the person Jim, is less sensitive to pain, he may have less fear of social rejection and therefore might approach more desirable potential romantic partners than a more sensitive peer might dare. Maybe the lower level of sensitivity means Jim is more outgoing and has more fulfilling relationships. Jim looks around his environment and sees opportunity, whereas someone with a body more sensitive to pain might look around and see greater risk of harm. This difference could fundamentally shift the way their two bodies respond to the same social environment, which will result, over time, in the creation of radically different selves. Jim could end up with a more desirable partner than a more sensitive person might, with a wider circle of friends, a more adventurous life. But Jim might also have more accidents that cause him or others harm; some people might find him insensitive to the needs of others or even reckless, both physically and emotionally. Now assume that we're no longer talking just about sensitivity, but many differences that occur across a number of features of our bodies.

We are not blank slates. But neither is our destiny determined solely by DNA. Selves, unique constellations of relationships and social interactions, also affect bodies. For example, lower social status, even among relatively egalitarian groups of farmer-foragers, is associated with higher levels of cortisol, a stress hormone that predicts negative health outcomes. Studies have also long shown that social isolation has negative health consequences. Even more surprising, there is evidence that the social environment can affect the expression of genes.[28,29] That is, the social environment can affect the operation of our physical body at its most basic level. The social world not only demands responses—whether fight or flight, say, in response to danger—it alters the instructions that determine the way our bodies exist in the world.

None of us are born into social vacuums. We come into existing relationships, multifaceted social dynamics, and broad cultural norms. These preexisting conditions give aspects of our physical body meaning. For example, sex at birth typically comes with a large suite of beliefs and expectations (e.g., performance of a specific gender) that affect our relationships before we open our eyes. Parents' ethnicity, language, and levels of income and education will have profound consequences for the self and life trajectory of their baby. We can predict a newborn's life outcomes with surprising accuracy given a bit of knowledge about the baby's parents. Some features of your life that will affect the construction of your self are determined before you're even born. In the United States, the neighborhood where a child is born strongly predicts their economic mobility.[30]

Yet, consider that a baby also has immense impact on others' selves, no matter the circumstances into which they are born. Not only do our bodies affect our selves, but our bodies affect the selves of others. A fetus begins to affect other selves before it's born. Partners might wonder how a new baby might change their relationships, their friends might think about fewer nights out, their parents likely begin preparing to become grandparents, a colleague might worry about the impending parent's leave. Each of these changes reflects a shift in relationships, which affects the selves of all those involved. In this way we see that the mere *idea* of a newborn begins to change the social fabric of those in its orbit well before the baby is born. The reordering of relationships and interactions puts pressure on the selves of prospective parents. And others in turn will be affected by the presumed changes that their children, friends, colleagues, and partners will undergo when they become parents.[31]

It's easy to see the far-reaching ripples and complex effects of a newborn. But I hope by the end of this book that I'll leave you with the understanding that each of our interactions, from childhood into old age, has ripple effects on our selves and others'. All selves push, pull, twist, and stretch the social structures they encounter.

2
—

# False Promises

"I am a sick man . . . I am a spiteful man," says the man hiding in the basement in Fyodor Dostoevsky's 1864 novel, *Notes from Underground*—considered by many to be the first fiction of existentialism. A midlevel bureaucrat, the narrator explains that his petitioners and superiors "tormented me to the point of shame, drove me to convulsions—I was so sick and tired of them in the end." He says that "excessive consciousness is a disease." What could inspire such thoughts? Our ability to see our self from an outsider's perspective and then to find the view unbecoming. It's painful to judge the self as a social creation and to find it lacking. This experience of a person's self-torment, expressed so accurately 160 years ago, is remarkably similar to the modern Western experience of self.

With all its self-aware neediness, empty bravado, self-pity, and fear, the modern self as portrayed by Dostoevsky isn't flattering. Still, it's easy to see a self-consciousness you might recognize. This man with no name is keenly aware of his self: the meaning of his choices, the possibilities of being. Indeed, his awareness leaves him paralyzed and ashamed, akin to a mouse living in a little hole.

Have you ever considered the many meanings of a decision to the point of paralysis? Have you ever had a thought that created a flush of embarrassment, followed by resentment or a moment of self-rebuke or loathing? These feelings, the man from underground tells us, are the disease of the modern person. And they have their root in a particular understanding of self: the self as an internal actor who looks out onto the world with its own, your own, singular view of reality.

It is easy to mistake this view of self as a recognition of reality, rather than just one way of thinking. People haven't always understood the self as we understand it now. It's tempting to think that our current understanding is more "evolved"—the idea of constant progress is comforting. But whether our collective understanding of self has progressed or not misses the point. What's important is that what constitutes self is not obvious.

THE CONTEMPORARY VERSION OF THE self seems to come with special powers. In 2007, Rhonda Byrne went on *The Oprah Winfrey Show* to discuss her recent bestselling book, *The Secret*. Over the course of two episodes the show pushed one very appealing idea: the Law of Attraction. According to Byrne, the Law of Attraction boils down to the idea that "you will produce what you think." Worry about being in the wrong place at the wrong time long enough, and you are likely to find yourself in an earthquake or a city torn apart by a hurricane. Truly believe that you will build a multimillion-dollar business, and it will happen. When describing why they believe in the Law of

Attraction—or "manifesting," as it's more often called today—
people interviewed in a *New York Times* article pointed to gain-
ing a sense of control in fraught times. "It can be a form of
self-soothing," a trend forecaster in New York said. "It's a way to
make sense of things in a moment where nothing makes sense."[1]
Trying to make sense of what is in fact senseless aligns well with
the central idea of *The Secret*, which came out right before the
Great Recession, an era of manifest loss.

It's worth noting how unusual a belief this is. Few in me-
dieval Europe would likely have believed their thoughts could
completely reshape their place in the world. A baker presumably
didn't believe he would or should become a blacksmith. The
feeling of freedom existed within a set of parameters that might
seem shockingly tight today.[2,3,4]

Nowadays, the idea seems to be that human potential, and
by extension your potential, is limitless. That the only barrier
to success is you. It's hard to imagine a more solipsistic view of
the world, one in which your reality is the *only* one that exists.
Your self is elevated to creator of reality. Wish it, believe it, and
it will be true. It's unclear how this works in a world where other
people wish for and believe things that contradict your wishes.
Whose thoughts become reality in that situation? We exist in
complex relationships with others. What if your multimillion-
dollar idea requires loans, but people who give loans don't give
them to people like you?

Byrne's idea—that we're in complete control of our lives—
can be seductive. It would be nice to believe that we can create
the world we want to live in if we just believe hard enough. If
things are going well for you, it's also nice to believe that this
reflects the reality you constructed. Doing great? Fantastic! You

deserve it because you made it a reality. No need to worry about potential injustices out there in the world or anything. Certainly there is no chance that you might have benefited from one or two of them. Now, if things aren't going so well for you, *The Secret* offers hope, but not much good advice, except to believe deeply that things will be better. It does, however, offer blame. Things not going well? You brought it on yourself. It certainly can't be the result of random events, complex social injustices, or something so mundane as other people's behavior. It can't be anything else outside of your control because *nothing* is outside of your control.

How did we get here, where millions and millions of people subscribe to the belief that their individual thoughts alone can transform the universe? What does all of this have to do with the way we think about self?

We experience self with such immediacy that it's hard to imagine anyone could question the sense of the self as we experience it. Yet the idea of self that we share, at least in the West, is not the only way people have ever thought about selves.

In Greco-Roman antiquity, for example, it's possible that they didn't share the uniquely "I"-focused understanding of self that we have today. Christopher Gill, a professor of ancient thought and author of two books on ancient Roman and Greek ideas of personality and self, goes so far as to suggest that it's arguable whether ancient Greeks and Romans "ever evolved the idea that selfhood is uniquely individual and 'I'-centered."

In his seminal study of the self through the history of autobiography, Karl Weintraub notes that St. Augustine's *Confessions*, written over three years starting in 397 CE, dwarfed any previous era's writing on the possibilities of a rich internal life. These days we aren't surprised when the author is the protagonist of their story, when the focus is the interiority of the writer. In contrast, Weintraub says of ancient Greeks and Romans, "In fundamental ways, often so hard for us who live in a highly differentiated society of individualists and individualities to understand, these earlier lives are enmeshed in and derive their meaning from basic social and kinship relations." The societies Gill studied and Weintraub described rooted a meaningful life in social interactions and communal relationships, rather than our modern focus on the self-contained, essential self, where fulfillment comes from turning internal desires into external reality through true belief. Maybe we have gone so far along the path of individualism that we can hardly imagine a self not defined by its internal life.

In the world described by Gill and Weintraub there was almost no room for a private self as we know it today. You would define yourself by kinship ties, social rank, and reputation, not by an internal sense of self, your personal values and attitudes. If you wanted to understand your self you would look outward to understand your place in your community, rather than inward. The idea that you could transcend your station, to ascend or descend to something other than what you were, might not have crossed your mind any more seriously than the thought of being a bird in flight. There would have been little sense in thinking of yourself as defined by an internal "personality."

This is far different from our current thinking about the self's almost magical power: an individual's ability to make their private thoughts into a new reality. We can understand the difference between the historical view and the dominant view today by thinking about the questions posed by the finger-wiggling exercise: Where is the line between internal and external? What is the essential self? In antiquity your place in the community was a constitutive part of your essential self. Who you were was defined by relationships within your community. Today many people think of their social relationships as external stimuli. We feel defined, instead, by our thoughts and feelings, which we think we know through introspection.[5,6,7,8]

In August 1976, *New York* magazine ran a cover with the title "The Me Decade," featuring a story by Tom Wolfe in which he claimed the 1970s ushered in a new attitude in America, away from collective good and toward self-interest. An economic boom influenced young people at the time to "take the money and run," he wrote, focusing on building better lives for themselves. Nearly thirty-seven years later, in May 2013, *Time* magazine ran a cover with the title "The Me Me Me Generation," accompanied by an image of a young girl looking at her phone. This time, the argument was that growing up with technology was influencing young people to become increasingly narcissistic. In both cases these covers were meant to describe a generational shift: a turn inward, a self-focus, a selfishness.

There is nothing new about the perceived connection between youth and selfishness, but our beliefs about self have changed over time.[9] In his book *Sources of the Self,* Charles Taylor suggests that the arts of the Renaissance foreshadowed the contemporary belief in the magic of selves. During this era, Taylor argues, artists moved toward a clearer imitation of nature. Painting and sculptures were intended to reflect reality. This placed artists at a remove: rather than part of the universe, Renaissance painters became an observer of their subject. As observers, individuals are outside of and unbound by the subject that they strive to capture—the artist becomes a godlike creator. Today, if Byrne is to be believed, we are all Renaissance artists, sitting above the world creating reality as we see it, or as we would like it to be. The self's existence does not depend on the social order. In this view, selves observe and manipulate or are observed and manipulated, but in any case, they *exist* independently of others.[10,11]

The self as understood today in the West arguably has its strongest roots in the Enlightenment views of self such as those expressed by René Descartes and later Immanuel Kant. From these perspectives the self is in each of our bodies and moral law is the product of human autonomy and reason.[12] In *Critique of Pure Reason*, Kant wrote, "All our knowledge begins with the senses, proceeds to the understanding, and ends with reason. There is nothing higher than reason."[13] The effects of this Enlightenment sense of self can perhaps be seen most clearly in the work and consequences of Adam Smith, a contemporary of Kant.

In 1776 Adam Smith wrote *An Inquiry into the Nature and Causes of the Wealth of Nations*.[14] Though he first used the phrase "invisible hand" in his book on selfhood and morality, *The Theory of Moral Sentiments*, the phrase is best known as a metaphor that explains, or justifies, modern economic thinking as expressed in *The Wealth of Nations*.[15] Smith's book is both a marker and a driver of a historical shift. Before the rise of capitalism, mercantilism was the dominant mode of economic relations between states, which focused on increasing each state's own exports while minimizing their imports. Thereafter, free markets driven by (individual) choice emerged as the modern (and near-global) economic system.

Self-interest—typically understood as the selfish nature

of *individuals*—is the basis of the modern economy. Modern understandings of Smith's invisible hand hew closely to the description provided by Paul Samuelson in his 1948 economics textbook. Samuelson wrote that "each individual in pursuing his own selfish good was led, as if by an invisible hand, to achieve the best good of all." The farmer who raises tomatoes, the driver who transports them, the grocer who stocks them, and everyone else from the seed distributor to the bagger are concerned with what's in it for them, not the enjoyment of others' salad or tomato sauce. The coordination among each of the actors who provided you ripe tomatoes: that's the invisible hand at work.[16]

As this individualistic conception of self evolves, its consequences reach far beyond the organization of the economy. Today it affects almost every aspect of our lives. The idea that children should have their own bedrooms; that bathrooms should be private; that our identities are, and should be, defined by personal choices, all these and more are the product of choices we've made based on a particular set of ideas about the world, rather than a reflection of the inescapable natural order of things.

With all this concern about individualism, you'd think we'd be able to pinpoint what it means to be an individual. What then is the thing in our bodies that is our *self*? We've considered the ideas of genetics and divine spirit. But here's another idea: the thing is our brain.

Today there is much faith placed in neuroscience and other physical sciences as the way to understand self. When you thought about the possibility of switching bodies, almost certainly you thought that your brain, or at least your neural activity, would be moved from your current body to someplace else. If you think of your self as your inner thoughts and feelings, it follows that you exist where you believe the components that define you exist, your brain.[17]

This idea, like all ideas, has a history. George H. W. Bush, the forty-first president of the United States, declared the 1990s to be the "Decade of the Brain." During this time neuroscientists, flush with cash and scientific excitement, made incredible advances. One such innovation was the widespread use of functional magnetic resonance imaging (fMRI), an imaging technique that uses extremely powerful magnets to monitor blood flow in the brain, which allows scientists to explore patterns of brain activation in real time. You could put someone in a machine and see changes in blood flow associated with brain activity: the more active a brain region, the more blood flowed to that part of the brain. Combined with a growing sense that we understood what happens in particular areas of the brain, the fMRI allowed us to literally see the brain working in real time.[18]

This ability to peer into the brain was irresistible to other disciplines, and the potential academic glory and money sloshing around for such work didn't hurt, either. A tremendous amount of research, across a range of disciplines, took a neuroscience approach to the exploration of human thought, decision making, and experience. Some social science departments bought multimillion-dollar machines, MRI machines for example, and hired people to operate them.[19,20]

Much of what happened, in my field of social psychology, during this period of intense focus on the brain was the (re)examination of classic work to identify where in the brain certain processes occurred. It seemed as if locating an experience in the brain gave the results more weight, as if we were discovering the truth of the experience that we had before only seen in people's outward behavior. It was as if, by looking at the brain, we were watching the little person work the controls, and as such, we could determine what the person was doing.

This way of thinking about self, reducing it to bodily processes, makes it easy to think about self in terms of a computer metaphor. If the body is nothing more than a biochemical machine, and the self is nothing more than a body, then machines can exist as our selves. In this way of thinking, our mind is software, and this software *is* self. Our physical body is the hardware we operate on. Using this metaphor, our selves can be copied, uploaded, or downloaded. Our selves, at least in theory, can exist indefinitely in infinitely upgradeable bodies.[21,22]

Even if you don't agree with this physically reductive view of *what* you are, you probably have the sense that you still know, at the very least, *who* you are. You know your deepest thoughts, hopes, dreams, and insecurities. You, and you alone, have direct access to your thoughts and feelings. But is that true?

As far as I know, no one can directly read your mind. The problem is that an inability to know someone else's internal cognitive processes might extend to include your inability to directly know your own. As Tim Wilson put it in his book *Strangers to Ourselves*, "research on the adaptive unconscious suggests that much of what we want to see is unseeable."[23] As we've discussed, the world is incredibly complex, certainly beyond our ability to understand at a conscious level, but it turns out that our ability to make sense of the world exceeds what we can access consciously. We can learn patterns and respond in strategic ways without conscious awareness of the pattern.

Imagine you are shown a screen with an array of numbers and letters in little boxes. Your job is to locate the number 6 as quickly as possible. Each time you locate it, a new array of numbers and letters appears and you do it again. Over time you get better at it; you start to find the 6 more quickly. It feels like you're faster because you are practicing, but in fact you're learning a pattern that's been programmed into the trials that helps you predict where the 6 will appear. How do we know it's not just practice? When the pattern is removed, speed declines immediately. Another interesting point is that the pattern is incredibly complex. So complex, in fact, that you can't consciously identify it and even if you could, you couldn't use it on purpose to increase your speed. How do we know you don't know it's there? The researchers who ran the study offered participants $100 to tell them what was going on and they couldn't. In fact, they also asked professors of psychology what they thought was happening and they couldn't identify that a pattern existed, either. To be clear, it's not that they couldn't describe the pattern—that would be unfair, because it's too complex for that—they didn't even know that a pattern was the reason they were getting faster at the task.[24,25]

When you think about it, this is incredible: we know more than we can consciously "see." The downside is that if you don't know how you do it, you often don't know that you're doing it at all. This also means that things you want to understand about your self might be beyond your ability to access. The feeling you have of direct access to your internal states might not be quite right.

You've certainly been in situations where someone's behavior has revealed something to you that the person might not have known about him- or herself. A light blush when you mention someone's name may clue you in that a friend is developing feelings for that person, even though your friend might not understand those feelings yet. It shouldn't take much to convince you of your imperfect understanding of the source of your thoughts, wants, or needs. Yet most of us have a strong sense of personal identity. Maybe we don't know where it comes from but we certainly have a sense that something stable is there.

David Hume, an eighteenth-century Scottish philosopher, suggested that this sense of personal identity is the result of two processes: resemblance and causation.[26] The first of these, resemblance, is the smooth, basically imperceptible shift from one thing to another. A new social interaction or small change in the structure of relationships changes the self, but the change might occur so smoothly or be so small as to go unnoticed as a change at all. Hume's second process, causation, is the sense that the complex interactions among elements driven by a common cause are experienced as a unity. Both views of identity have significant implications for the proposed model of self.

Resemblance, according to Hume, is evidence that memory "not only discovers identity, but also contributes to its production." This is a deeply psychological understanding of personal identity. The sense of who we've been, and who we are, is constructed from bits and pieces of the past filtered through our memories. Memories work like the game of telephone: one person starts a message that's passed verbally from person to person and ends the cycle at best a garbled version of the original message, and at worst something unrecognizable.

Our memory is flexible enough to induce people to remember things that didn't happen. Studies have induced adolescents to remember committing a crime that never happened and adults to falsely remember events from childhood. Memories are not faithful recordings that we can pull from our experience on command. Memories are influenced by events that intervene between the experience and our attempt to recall it.[27,28] We change and so can our memories. So if your sense of self depends on recall of the characteristics and stories that make you uniquely you, the experience of reflecting on yourself might be one of bringing the self to mind. But because memories are not faithful recordings, if you believe you are your memories, each experience of the self is a new creation. You are reborn every time you call your self to mind.

The idea of resemblance, coupled with the fact that you spend every waking moment with your self, creates a difference between the way you experience your self and the way you experience others. As you think of your self it is more difficult to recognize changes because you often move from one state to the other in tiny steps at a time. When I talked earlier of a friendly argument with a colleague about having changed her mind and therefore her self, she retorted it wasn't like I changed her from an introvert to an extrovert—she was arguing resemblance. I might have had a small effect on one belief of many, but this change was just an itsy-bitsy thing, too inconsequential to count as a change in her self. But Hume's point is that because changes are often small and incremental, we don't see our selves changing. From our perspective slow evolution isn't experienced as a shift in self. Continuous exposure to our selves makes it difficult to see change, and this is mistaken for evidence that change has not occurred.

You probably have had the experience of seeing people after a long absence and noting with surprise how much they have physically changed, maybe their hair thinned, maybe crow's feet crept into the corners of their eyes, maybe they put on weight, but the change is jarring. The time between meetings can break the illusion of continuity. It allows us to be startled by the amount of change we see in others, sometimes exaggerated by the feeling that we have changed less during the same time.

EARLIER, I ARGUED THAT YOUR self is a construction of your social environment—where and when you grew up and where you are in the moment. Even how much you care to explore your self, or "find yourself" as some might say, is influenced by when and where you were born. In the United States, some connect the modern obsession with our search for a "true self" to movements of the 1960s and '70s. Hippies, the human potential movement, "new age" spirituality—these things were in part a response to the social milieu of the preceding decades: consumerism and conformity.[29]

To some of these new thinkers, conforming to societal norms and expectations—moving to the suburbs for the house and white picket fence, having a few kids and a dog, participating mindlessly in the civil life of the neighborhood—was stifling the self. The self, in their view, was only seen in the absence of oppressive influences, among them wage labor, materialism, and other supposedly stale social conventions. Among a segment of the population, the sixties was the era of free love. In his book on the sixties cultural revolution, John McWilliams described hippies as "shunning Christianity, monogamy, conventional dress, and private property."[30]

At Esalen, a retreat center along the Northern California coast considered by many the center of the human potential movement, academics and spiritual seekers, physicists and psychologists were exploring a "no religion" style of religion associated with traditions from Asia. In his book on the history of Esalen, Jeffrey Kripal, a professor of philosophy and religious thought at Rice University, described it as a place that "chose to operate with modern democratic principles, individualist values, a celebration of science, secular notions of religion as a primarily private affair of personal choice and creativity, and socially liberal agendas."[31]

In a somewhat different approach, Ayn Rand, a popular philosopher at the time, advocated selfishness as a moral good, but clarified that to be selfish was not to do whatever you want, but to act for your own rational self-interest. She wrote of this philosophy most famously in her dystopian novel *Atlas Shrugged*, which explores the consequences to the world if all creative thinkers, business leaders, and scientists went on strike. She called her philosophy Objectivism, a set of ideas that elevated the individual and often licensed ignoring the needs of others and the value of community standards.

This elevation of the personal self, the individual's needs and wants, over social concerns is a pretty close cousin to contemporary understandings of Adam Smith: once individuals are free to pursue selfish ends, all are bettered—we produce more, more cheaply, so the quality of (material) life is raised for all. For Smith and Rand, the world would grow richer and people's lives would be improved; for some in the sixties counterculture, the world could be healed.

When you believe that the self is defined individually—and when we elevate the needs of that self—you can end up both demonizing external constraints and glorifying selfish striving.

Since individualism was already the rock of capitalist thinking, it doesn't take much to see the sixties view of self morph from something counterculture to something quite mainstream. It's a short trip from "turn on, tune in, drop out" to "greed is good."

Even though the vision of self that was lionized by the movements of the sixties was a sharp contrast to the prevailing mood that immediately preceded it, the romantic idea of an individual self to be discovered and nurtured is nothing new. Ralph Waldo Emerson, after all, believed that "nothing can bring you peace but yourself."[32] And since at least Rousseau, many thinkers have built a utopian ideal on the foundational belief that humans are fundamentally good in their natural state. The Romanticism of Rousseau was in part a reaction to the rationalism associated with the Age of Reason. Rousseau and other Romantics emphasized the individual, the imaginative, the personal, and the emotional. In some Romantics' minds, the natural state is one of freedom from outside forces that corrupt us.[33,34,35]

It seems people, at least today, might be natural Romantics, in that many of us believe moral behaviors stem from a person's "true self." Research suggests that we believe immoral behavior is the aberration to be explained. We seem to think that if people were allowed to be their true selves, they would be good—the essence of our selves is equivalent to our positive moral characteristics and anything "bad" is due to something outside our "true" selves.[36,37,38]

As YOU MIGHT HAVE GUESSED by now, I personally reject the idea that anyone has an innate "true self." The idea that moral behavior is internal and therefore captures our true self, while immoral behavior merely reflects external influences, assumes first that people can distinguish between internal and external forces. And as we've seen, this might not be as easy as we imagine. The belief in a true self also suggests sole ownership of some actions—moral actions. As should be clear by this point, my argument is that to have a self at all requires others. But it's not enough to have others around: you have to *accept* and *know* others are around. This might sound like a distinction without difference. If others are around, surely you know that's the case. But it turns out that doesn't have to be true. Humans have the ability to dehumanize their fellow human beings, to deny their humanity. The word *dehumanization* sounds intensely negative and it can be. Dehumanization is, after all, often a critical component of genocide: people described as vermin can also be described as an infestation that must be eradicated.

But dehumanization can also look like treating someone as inconsequential. Think about how often people in service roles might be treated as inconsequential—people call a car and don't really register the driver, people barely notice the person who pours them water at the restaurant. At some point, we all have probably failed to recognize the full humanity of someone we encountered.[39,40,41]

It's an active process to recognize others. It's not the mere physical presence of other *Homo sapiens* that makes us fully human, but the recognition of our shared humanity.

Where does this leave us? First, the self is a complex idea. To say you know your self or understand your self often underestimates the complexity of self.

Second, the self is not a thing that sits there in the world to be understood. Humans create the idea of self, and as such it is subject to change.

Third, the *idea* of self matters. It affects the way we engage with the world, and as such is tightly tied to the way the world is organized.

# 3

## Freedom, Really?

*What is it that every person pursues? To be in
a good condition, to be happy, to do everything
as he wishes, not to be frustrated, not to be put
under compulsion.*

—Epictetus

What is it to be free? Why does this idea inspire and justify actions as momentous as protest at risk of imprisonment or worse or, even more extreme, national declarations of war? It seems like the word *freedom* bestows magical properties, giving everything attached to it the patina of righteousness: political freedom, academic freedom, freedom of speech, religious freedom. To attach freedom to an idea raises the idea above reproach. It's as if freedom purifies all that it touches. Conversely, to be denied freedom is a fate considered worse than death. The state motto of New Hampshire is "Live Free or Die"—apparently, a life without freedom is worse, at least in New Hampshire, than no life at all.

We saw this play out on a large scale during the COVID-19 pandemic. Many people considered mask and vaccine mandates an encroachment on their freedom and, in rebelling against these rules, those very same people may have contributed to their own death or the death of others.

The concept of *freedom*, when used in phrases like "Live Free or Die," is like the word *love*—it captures a human longing, a primal need, that's difficult to nail down with precision. It's the sort of thing that people have in mind when they say, "You know it when you see it." But this is not enough for our purposes.

To understand the relationship between self and freedom we need to dive a bit deeper into the idea and definition of freedom. The idea of freedom has long been the founding principle for how societies, at least Western ones, should be organized, what it takes to live a good life, and the relationship between humans and the divine. To really get at the importance of freedom we need to think about three questions: 1) What does it mean to be free? 2) Can we be free? and, 3) Do we want to be free? This book can be read in part as a meditation on the third question—"Do we want to be free?"—and the consequences of our answers. My answer to that question is "not really," or at least "not completely."

I realize it's not fair to tell you that in actuality you *don't* want to be completely free without first being clear about what I mean by freedom. When people use the word *freedom*, they typically have something in mind like, *The right to do or say what I want without someone stopping me*. When people talk about freedom in this way, my sense is that they mean something more than a simple reading of this definition. To give a better sense of what I have in mind when I talk about freedom, I am going to break this definition into three parts: "the right to do or say," "what you want," and "without someone stopping you." Let's explore them in reverse order.[1]

When I think about my freedom being taken away, I generally think about someone stopping me from living my life the way I would like to. That can be as simple as my partner demanding that we see a particular movie, and as complex as limitations—in housing, work opportunities, feeling safe, and more—because of the color of my skin. To give you an example of the latter, I'll recall an incident that happened to me when I was about seventeen years old in the early 1990s. One afternoon I drove with a friend to pick up his buddy who was going to give us both a haircut. It was a sunny afternoon in Chicago, and we were driving on a pretty relaxed street, tree-lined with manicured lawns. I parked the car and my friend hopped out to ring his buddy's bell. While I was waiting, a police car turned onto the street a ways down the block. Two officers got out of their car and frisked a group of guys hanging out on the corner. As far as I could tell they didn't find anything because they let all the guys go a moment later. I watched all of this from inside my car, uninvolved and only vaguely interested, until the police started walking toward my car, hands on their guns, and demanded that I get out.

As I stepped out of the car, with a calm "What's the problem, Officer?," my friend and his buddy were walking toward me. One of the officers pushed my friend onto the hood of my car, frisked him, and again found nothing. They asked me and my friend's buddy to stand against the car, and then they asked if they could search my pockets. I calmly said no. The officer said if I didn't consent to the search he was going to take me in. After refusing again, I was handcuffed and put in the back of the patrol car. My car was searched and impounded. I was taken in, charged with resisting arrest, and held until early the next morning.

In that moment the police limited my freedom in obvious ways. The police took away my freedom of movement when they handcuffed me and to an even greater extent when they put me in the patrol car and then later a holding cell. They also prevented me from getting a haircut, and disrupted everything else I had planned for the day.

But I'd argue these are only the most visible impingements on my freedom. If they had never restrained me, but only treated me with suspicion and disrespect, that too would have taken something from me. They would have impaired my sense of safety in the presence of representatives of the very institution purported to keep citizens safe, the police. They would have taken from me the sense that I am respected in society.

Many mostly Black and Brown men have had much the same experience as I did that day. In fact, it's part of this country's political legacy to allow such things to occur, in the name of public safety. In the 1990s, the New York City Police Department began extensive use of what is known as a stop-and-frisk policy. Between 2002 and 2019, more than 5 million people were stopped for dubious cause(s) and forced to endure a search and questioning. These interrogations rarely led to the discovery of illegal or dangerous contraband—more than 90 percent of those stopped were innocent. Yet each of these stops took a bit of someone's freedom: the freedom to walk the street without fear of official harassment.[7]

When we think about "someone stopping" us from doing what we want, it's easy to think only in terms of police stopping you or patting you down, but that's a particularly narrow view of the situation. Much of society is structured hierarchically; some people are afforded more power than others. Sometimes hierarchies are created purposefully and transparently to achieve an agreed-upon goal, for example formal organizational hierarchies. And sometimes hierarchies are the result of individuals' or groups' exploitation of the vicissitudes of nature or history. Almost certainly you have had the experience of having your freedom curtailed by someone who had more power than you. Perhaps your boss asked you to complete a project that encroached on your weekend, maybe someone bigger or stronger than you just pushed you out of the way, or maybe a political party used its influence to enact a law that limits your freedom.[3]

When I was a kid, there was a bully in my neighborhood. He was older and larger than me and my friends and would threaten us with violence for sport. I remember times we stayed on the front porch when we feared he might be nearby. For all we knew, he might not have been outside or even in our city. It was enough for us to know that there was a *possibility* of harm to keep us from venturing out. Now, instead of a child with a behavioral issue carrying a stick, imagine a police force with guns. Each instance of stop-and-frisk was a threat to both those who were stopped *and* those who worried they might be. In fact, the stop-and-frisk program was *designed* as a threat, a bludgeon to freedom.

Threats are not the only way to limit someone's freedom without physical intervention. What if someone offered you $1 million, or $10 million, to engage in some relatively easy task.

Would you say no? The term *golden handcuffs* was coined to describe compensating people so handsomely that it becomes difficult for them to leave the organization. Being made an offer you can't refuse. Being proposed to by someone rich and attractive, but boring and not very bright. People have needs and desires, as well as fears. If you accept that fear can diminish the ability to do or say what you want, can't needs and desires do the same?

There is also a loss of freedom associated with what you *do* in accordance with those wants and needs. If you do a thing because I pay you to do it, you lose the opportunity to have done something else. If you have ten dollars and I manipulate you to spend it on one thing, I've stopped you from spending it on something else. Advertisements are designed to part you from your money. For example, they might try to get you to buy a car by convincing you that people will find you more attractive if you drive a certain make and model. Maybe you've seen the ads where good-looking, well-dressed people turn their heads to look at the driver in the shiny new car the ad is selling. Whether I explicitly stop you from doing a thing or induce you to do a thing, I've reduced your freedom. There are fewer options after you encounter me than there were before.

With a more expansive understanding of the idea of "someone stopping you," freedom is now on more precarious ground. Much of what we do or say is affected by the demands of others. Sometimes people blatantly violate our ability to do or say what we want through violence or fear. Sometimes they manipulate our needs and desires, as through ads or directly offering us something we need, like a paycheck. And sometimes their mere presence creates obligation—think of parents whose freedom is drastically curtailed by the arrival of their helpless little new-borns.[4] If freedom requires the absence of external influences, it's not at all clear that it's possible to live freely. As we will see, it's not clear that you would *want* to live "free" of external influences, even if you could.

To live life as you would like requires knowing what you want in the first place. Let's say you've found a way to sidestep the influence of others. Then what does it mean to do "what you want"? This might seem a smaller impediment to freedom than avoiding external influence. But like many things in life, it's more complicated than it seems.

*Want* is a funny word. What do we mean when we say we want something? If you're hungry I assume you want to eat, but what if you don't want to feel hungry? What if you're dieting and are trying to limit your calories? In that situation, do you want to eat? An idea of freedom that only focuses on external barriers to behavior is terribly shortsighted. Some of your greatest demons, the biggest impediments to the life you want to live, might be choices you make seemingly freely, or at least without external constraint. The feeling of freedom is a bit more complicated, in other words, than access to short-term hedonistic action. As I write this, I am drinking a cup of coffee. The coffee helps me get in the right mood to write. I wanted a cup of coffee. More accurately, I wanted to get these words down on the page and thought coffee would help. This is as good an explanation for my coffee drinking as any, but is it true?

If you're someone who drinks coffee every morning, you might say you want coffee, when what you really mean is you *need* coffee. If you need coffee and can get it without anyone stopping you, are you free? You are free to drink coffee, but I doubt that's what people mean when they talk about freedom. What if instead of coffee, you needed heroin?

You can be free to indulge a destructive addiction, but I don't think that most people would call the ability to satisfy a compulsion that they would rather not have freedom. Whether compulsion is internal or external doesn't change that it's a compulsion, and people don't typically consider actions they feel that they can't control free.

None of us are perfect. Sometimes we drink more than we think we should, we eat poorly, stay up later than we think we should. We are not coerced to do these things, but we also don't think they are best for us. Sometimes it's a struggle to do the right thing. When we struggle and fail, when we don't do what we think we should, are we free?

If by freedom we mean the ability to do what we think is right for us, there is another hurdle we must confront. When we think about what's right for us, what self do we have in mind? What I think is right for me as a son and what's right for me as a man might not be the same thing. When we move beyond thinking of the self in physical terms, this question becomes crucial.

To complicate matters further, the needs, desires, and fears of each of our selves don't have to and may not align. As a man, I might feel the need to stand up for myself and others. I might need to feel and appear strong. As a son, I might need to show deference to my mother and be mindful of her concerns for me.

During my run-in with the police, was my behavior—the refusal to be searched—what was right for me?

Think of me as a son. I might share a reality with my mother that police officers are a danger to avoid or mollify. Yet, for some reason I challenged the officers' authority. From this vantage, you could argue that I didn't do what I thought was best for me, and therefore I wasn't free.

Now think of me as a man. Depending on my definition of manhood, my self might demand that I push back in the face of injustice. From this perspective, my behavior was a manly reaction to a violation of my basic rights. From this perspective, I acted freely. These examples provide a simple way to see that not only do relationships define our selves, they also affect our experience of freedom.

I draw different conclusions when I think about my behavior as that of a son than when I think about the same behavior as that of a man. The story we tell about our behavior depends on our current perspective. Our understanding of our behavior depends on the self we inhabit while in the situation—recall the different selves of the Asian-American women taking a math test—and the ability to interpret our behavior as free or not is as complicated as the relationships that define us.

In my interaction with the police I could have been enacting a self that was defined by my relationship with my mother. This might sound strange because the way I behaved was probably not what my mother would have wanted. How could I have behaved as my mother's son, even though I knew my mother wouldn't have wanted me to act the way I did? Well, my mother strongly believes in standing up for what's right, and because I saw the instance of the police stop as relevant to that belief, the standing up for myself may have come from my mother, even though as a parent she might not have wanted her son to behave as I did.

The irony is that there is no reason to suppose that a self defined by a relationship with a particular person—say, your mother—will behave in ways that satisfy that person. In fact, it's possible that the maintenance of a valued relationship constrains you to conflict within that very relationship. Imagine that "you," as defined by the relationship with your parents, value independence. Your parents always wanted to raise an independent child, and early on pushed you to make decisions for yourself. They told you that you never had to go along with what others wanted from you. If an adult relative wanted a hug, an innocuous and common behavior in your extended family, you could say no without repercussion. Over time all of this worked: you grew up to be someone who jealously protected your ability to ignore the demands of others, a version of your self created in your relationship with your parents. This outcome, however, could easily create conflict. Maintaining that relationship requires that you see your self as independent, which might require rejecting your parents' wants or demands. Maybe your parents want grandchildren, and they keep bringing it up. If you've decided not to have kids, or at least not for the time being, to be your independent self, the self created in the relationship with your parents, requires you to disappoint your parents.

This highlights two aspects of self as it relates to freedom. First, you don't necessarily choose which self you inhabit in any given situation. The social situation elicits a self; you dance to the tune that's being played. Second, the behaviors associated with a given self need not reflect your acceptance of others' views (a parent, partner, coworker, friend, etc.), but you will be affected by these views.

In my interaction with the police the die was cast early on. The opening of the interaction, the approach with hands on guns, giving commands, started the interaction down a certain path. I didn't see myself as the officers did. But I was certainly affected by their view. Whenever I encounter a police officer today, even as a Stanford professor, the possibility that they experience me as a threat to them or society is the first thing on my mind. This also tells me something about my place in American society, about who I am in this country.

SOMETIMES, AS IN MY EXPERIENCE with the police, the actions of others restrict our freedom. But sometimes those restrictions actually come from our selves. We all know when what we're doing feels like a compulsion rather than a choice. If you've ever had to ask for a bathroom break you know what I mean. Almost everyone considers their body's basic physical needs (air, food and drink, sleep, etc.) compulsory. The focus on the body might also lead you to think of physical needs we develop as addictions (e.g., heroin, nicotine, caffeine). But as you move further away from the biological and toward the psychological, people are probably less likely to label a given behavior an addiction. For example, people might not agree that an outsize appetite for status or power is an addiction.

This line between compulsion and choice is fascinating, and far less sharp than you might imagine. Certainly, you have felt your freedom affected by fear, say, of failure or rejection or by psychological needs and desires, say, to make a lot of money or to impress your friends. If you have an intense fear of heights, how likely are you to go skydiving? You could—no one is stopping you—but it's extremely unlikely. You stop yourself. As a social psychologist, I find these experiences—the times when features of your self drive your behavior—to be the most interesting.

Going back to my interaction with the officers, was I free

when I refused to comply with them? The answer to the question depends on which version of me refused to comply. I could say I chose, and thus was free, if my behavior was aligned with what I thought was best for me in the moment. In this instance it could be that as a man I chose freely, but as a son I did not. If freedom is doing what is best for you, to know whether an action is free or not requires we know which self acted.

The existence of multiple selves raises another hurdle for the idea of individual freedom. I assume you have a sense of what's right for each of your selves, but where does this sense of right and wrong come from? If exposure to "perfect" bodies portrayed in movies and advertisements drives your desire to diet and work out, are you free because no one is stopping you from doing something you think is good for you? Or are you being driven by insecurities, desire for approval, or vanity—all of which are fueled by those images? We all exist in a cultural context that shapes what we think we should want and how we think we should behave.

In December 2007 a young woman named Amy Carlson left her husband and three kids and moved to the mountains in Colorado. Two years later, she and her new "mountain man," Amerith WhiteEagle, released the first video on a YouTube channel that would eventually host 2,700 of their videos, where the group spouted conspiracy theories and explained how Mother God would save humanity. As of September 2021, the group had nearly 20,000 Facebook followers and almost 10,000 subscribers on YouTube. Carlson named her organization Love Has Won, at first telling followers that they were loved unconditionally and giving tips for accessing one's inner joy. Dozens of followers moved to Colorado with Carlson (WhiteEagle soon left the community), who claimed she was the reincarnation of famous historical figures like Joan of Arc, Cleopatra, Marilyn Monroe, and, most notably, Jesus. She called herself Mother God, claiming that she processed the world's "negative energy" and that she had an enemy in a global organization called the Cabal. The Cabal was allegedly responsible for everything from international wars to mass shootings and even the COVID-19 pandemic, all in an attempt to keep people in constant fear.

Amy's followers, both those who lived with her and those online, believed she would help them ascend to a higher "5D" plane of existence, so they would be saved when the broken 3D world was destroyed. Followers were encouraged to release their "3D relationships," leaving family and friends behind to join Love Has Won. Members took on various roles in the organizational structure of Love Has Won, which was named a 501(c)(3) nonprofit charity in 2019. They would livestream videos, write blog articles, perform online consultations, and sell essential oils, crystal pyramids, and colloidal silver through a business called Gaia's Whole Healing Essentials.

Although all of this might sound wild from the outside, the members of Love Has Won truly believed they were fighting a great battle for the fate of humanity. That they alone knew the truth of the 3D world.[5,6] From the outside, we might see this community as a cult, and some may consider members of the community "brainwashed." By this, people mean that these members are not acting freely; they are under someone else's control. If we assume that members aren't staying in the group due to threats of violence, describing members' behavior as the product of brainwashing is curious. If they are deciding to stay based on the social context of the cult, aren't we all in some version of the same situation? We are all, in the end, making sense of and responding to the social reality we inhabit.

We are all sensitive to the beliefs and ideas of those around us. People's ideas about right and wrong, in particular, are influenced by their social environments. Consider the fact that there have been cultures in which it was morally appropriate to hunt other human beings. In the United States, not that long ago, large groups of people attended lynchings as family outings— they took photos, which you can see online today, and sent them as postcards. Sometimes they even took pieces of the victim's body as souvenirs.[7]

Alternatively, there have also been societies in which people would not allow a member of their village to go hungry if anyone had food.[8,9]

Over time, the collective idea of what's right and wrong in a community shifts. At this very moment, you and I might accept ideas and engage in behaviors that years from now could be seen as reprehensible: eating meat despite the suffering of animals, driving cars despite the deaths that inevitably result, maybe even taking a shower despite the knowledge of limited potable water. These and a slew of other things that might seem completely innocuous could come to be seen as immoral by the majority of society. If there aren't powerful voices raising alarms, if friends and family tell us these actions are fine, then for most of us, these things *are* fine. Remember, the more people with whom you share a world and its attendant norms, the saner you seem, regardless of the content of that world.

To further complicate things, we might not even have access to what is driving our sense of right and wrong. We might believe we have chosen what's in fact been given. As we discussed in Chapter 1, we can't just look in our heads or hearts to locate the source of our beliefs.

We seem to have a particularly hard time seeing things clearly when we don't like what we see. We have the curious tendency to think we know our selves less well after engaging in behavior we consider immoral. In a study published in 2016, researchers asked people to indicate whether they had ever engaged in a list of 20 commonplace behaviors typically considered immoral (e.g., lying to one's parents). On average, participants indicated having engaged in about 10 of the 20 behaviors listed. Another group completed the same questionnaire, but with a list of commonplace "moral" behaviors (e.g., returning a valuable item, rather than keeping it). In this case, on average people listed having engaged in about 18 of the 20 behaviors.[10]

But here's the interesting part: the researchers also asked the people to report their degree of self-knowledge. People in the immoral condition reported knowing their selves less well. It seems that people have a hard time understanding their self when viewed as the source of immoral behavior.

Social psychologists distinguish between what people believe drives their behavior and the way things actually work. We know that you can't trust people's stories about why they do what they do or even where their ideas come from. It's not that people lie, it's that they often try to figure out why they do what they do after the act is done. People try to make sense of themselves the same way they try to make sense of others.

It might be that the feeling of your self as a singular, continuous, and coherent being that you know and understand is a useful fiction. This version of you might be the protagonist of the story you make of your life. Our sense of right and wrong, composed of influences we have only the barest sense of, helps us weave a story from the disparate threads and random events that compose (and even predate) our lives.[11,12]

We've already taken a deeper look into what it means for "someone to stop you," or what it means to "want something," noting how these actions and desires complicate our ideas of freedom, broadly defined: *the right to do or say what I want without someone stopping me.* This brings us to the "do or say" component of freedom. The seeming simplicity of "doing" and "saying" might underestimate what we want from freedom. "Doing" and "saying" are ways to reveal or, more accurately, create who we are. If you fancy yourself someone who enjoys adventure, there's a good chance you spend time and money on travel, maybe to exotic locations or doing extreme activities. Perhaps rather than an ability to "do or say," what we really want is the ability to *be* what we want without someone stopping us. Maybe true freedom is the ability to self-define, the freedom to decide who and what we are.

With a better understanding of what I mean by freedom, let's turn back to the question of whether people really want to be free in the first place. It's certainly true that people don't like being told what they can and can't do. When people believe others are trying to control them, they often respond by trying to assert their autonomy. For example, in 1987 in most of the United States it became illegal for people younger than twenty-one to consume alcohol. A study of alcohol consumption soon after found that younger students who were now not legally able to drink consumed more than older students. The sense that their freedom to drink was curtailed pushed them to consume more.[13]

I'm sure you can easily bring to mind an instance in which someone tried to control what you could or couldn't say or do. I'll go out on a limb and say you didn't like it. Suddenly my claim that people don't really want freedom sounds ridiculous. Yes, explicit attempts to limit your freedom can elicit resistance. This requires that you understand that people are *trying* to limit you. But that can be hard to see clearly. For example, few people interpret the simple act of being in a relationship as an attempt to limit them.

Human beings are social creatures. We seek out relationships and every relationship affects what you can be. We need relationships and willingly accept—often willingly embrace—the influence that comes along with these relationships. My point is that people might believe they want the ability to be and behave in accord with what they think is best for them without external interference, yet their behavior doesn't bear this out.

Throughout our evolutionary history, without relationships, without communities, humans would not have survived. To be cast out of society was akin to a death sentence. Today, in the modern world, there are very, very few products that an individual uses that can be produced without the contribution of hundreds, if not many thousands, of others in long supply chains that span the globe. Consider the complexity of creating and transporting any modern technological device. Even if we put aside our material needs, without social contact human beings suffer significant mental and physical decline. Consequently, knowingly and unknowingly, we give up freedom to satisfy these needs. The relationships that sustain us also make demands of us. They simultaneously expand us and limit us. They tell us who we are and who we can and cannot be.

# PART II

# You

## *and*

# Them

# 4

—

# Hugs and Straitjackets

The *Epic of Gilgamesh* is a poem that was found by archaeologists in modern-day Iraq in 1849 among the ruins of the library of Ashurbanipal—a major king of the Assyrian Empire. The poem has been found inscribed on clay tablets in Sumerian, Akkadian, and Babylonian. The Sumerian fragments, the oldest, date to about 2000 BCE. In part, the poem tells the story of two extraordinary beings in what I would consider a beautiful but in many ways ordinary relationship.

The story revolves around a king, Gilgamesh, a being two-thirds divine and one-third mortal. He is described as about eighteen feet tall and strong beyond measure. Gilgamesh lives as he pleases. He is free from concern about the expectations of others; he is free to act without anyone stopping him. And as he indulges in this freedom, he terrorizes the citizens of his city, Uruk.

Tired, fearful, and unable to defend themselves from Gilgamesh's unchecked appetites, the citizens beg the gods to rein in Gilgamesh's excesses. Presumably the gods could have sapped his strength or struck him down, but instead they created a partner for Gilgamesh: Enkidu, a man designed to be his equal. When Enkidu learns of Gilgamesh's treatment of the citizens of Uruk, he decides to put an end to it. The two engage in a titanic fight that splinters doorways and shakes walls. Ultimately, Gilgamesh prevails. When Enkidu admits defeat the two embrace and become fast friends. Presumably, each recognizes some of himself in the other, which creates mutual respect. And with that Gilgamesh's behavior shifts. We no longer hear of him tormenting the citizens of Uruk. His relationship with Enkidu changes him.

In this, one of the earliest examples of human literature, we already see an understanding of the power of relationships. Gilgamesh is constrained not by ropes or chains; the gods change him through the development of a friendship. The unknown poets' decision to use Enkidu to constrain Gilgamesh reveals an understanding that relationships change us, and in doing so cost us a bit of our freedom.

At the beginning of your life your sense of self is diffuse, inchoate, not particularly well defined. When you are a child, you might imagine becoming an astronaut, a ballet dancer, a basketball player, a parent. Over the ensuing years, as you engage in relationships and have interactions of all kinds, a self comes into better focus, which also means that uncertainty and possibilities are diminished. If you've ever had to move for work, think about where you decided to live. I have a friend who is pretty liberal, and so was her best friend. Her friend moved to a different part of the state, which happened to be more conservative. She made new friends and joined a new church in the area, and soon my friend started to notice changes. Her friend began to adopt more conservative views that created more and more distance within their friendship. Eventually, they completely lost touch.

Even as adults, who we are around changes us. The people in our social orbit affect the way we dress, speak, and view the world. Our lives are driven by a large ensemble of players, both on- and offstage. Experiences with your family likely taught you what it means to be a good daughter or son and brother or sister; experiences at school and work have taught you how to be a good friend or coworker. But consider a brand-new friendship. When you meet a new friend you don't arrive alone. You bring all your other relationships with you. At this point in my life, if you met me you would be affected by others in close orbit around me: my partner, my sister, some of my work colleagues, and a handful of close friends. Who I am is always in flux and these people are consistent influences on the way I see and engage the world. The same is true for you, for better or worse; there are people in your life, past and present, who influence who you are and will be if we meet. Who you are, or were, in those relationships shapes who you can become in a new relationship. And who you become in this new relationship will also affect who you are in your existing relationships.

Every relationship makes a demand of you; they demand that you play your part. We all co-construct the reality that constitutes the play of our lives, and in doing so we continually make and remake the selves, including our own, that are the players. During my interaction with the police, those officers and I created a reality. The police saw me as a potential law-breaker, which required something of them—that they treat me with suspicion and some degree of fear because they didn't trust me to behave as a law abiding citizen. Once I understood this view, I engaged with them as unjust authorities, which required something of me. It required that I resist their requests. In this situation, they and I had clarity about our selves. We played out a tragedy in our shared reality. They read their lines and I read mine.

I highlight my interaction with the police because it helps clarify what I'm talking about when I talk about freedom. I'm not just talking about freedom from perceived hindrances to what you want to do. It's true that the police officers took a sort of freedom from me when they handcuffed me, but that's not the important issue for us here. As the interaction unfolded, many branches of possibilities were pruned. The interaction diminished possibilities of what I could be in that moment as well as what I could be in the future. The experience might have reduced my trust in authority figures. Maybe it increased my vigilance about injustice. In whatever way it changed me, I can never be a person who didn't have that experience.

My long-ago interaction with the police was negative for many reasons, but it also reflects truths about relationships. In every relationship we define each other. This can be a terrible or a beautiful thing, but it is unavoidable. On that day I could have been an academically gifted high school student and respected by police officers—officers trusted to serve and protect people like me. As a statement of fact, that could have been as true as what transpired. The police officers could also have been people who worked with law-abiding citizens, like me, to make everyone safer.

But in the interaction none of those selves were created; in fact, we eliminated them as possibilities. The interaction limited us, and in so doing created clarity. We all knew the parts we were expected to play. From my perspective, I was the innocent but wronged citizen, and they were the racist cops. From their perspective, I was the potentially violent threat to society, and they were the protectors of society.

THE COMPLEXITIES AND COSTS OF some interactions might be enough to make you wonder if less isn't more. You might be tempted to think you are better off limiting interactions with others to avoid the ones that go poorly. If I hadn't been on the street that day with my friend, I wouldn't have had that encounter with the police. It's easy to underestimate the need for social connection when it's always available, but when opportunities to connect contract, the depth of the need comes into sharper focus.

People all over the world got personal experience with this when the COVID-19 pandemic forced us to stay home, seeing friends and family only through screens or on the other side of glass windows. But even without something as dramatic as a worldwide pandemic, it's easy to see evidence for the need to connect. In a study published in 2009 by two Australian researchers, participants were asked to spend ten to fifteen minutes writing about a personal experience of social inclusion, social exclusion, or just an everyday experience. Then they all were given a list of positive and negative traits uniquely tied to human nature (e.g., active, curious, impatient, nervous) and were asked to rate themselves and the person who excluded or included them on these dimensions. After exclusion, people rated the person who excluded them *and* themselves as having fewer human nature traits.[1]

When we feel excluded, we see people who excluded us *and*

ourselves as less human. It might not surprise you to hear that we deny others their humanity when we feel ignored by them, but the fact that we rate ourselves as having fewer human traits is more telling. At some level we understand that our humanity depends on recognition from others.

In another study researchers had people play a simple computer game where three people threw a ball to each other. In some cases, everyone had the ball thrown to them about the same number of times. But in other cases, one person was never thrown the ball. The researchers wanted to know whether social exclusion would make the person not thrown the ball more likely to try to fit in a later task. To get at this, after the game participants were asked to complete a "perceptual task." After watching six other people answer a question incorrectly, the person previously not thrown the ball was more likely than people who had been thrown the ball to go along with the crowd and give the incorrect answer, presumably to fit in.[2]

After feeling socially excluded, people are more likely to conform. Why? Because humans have a deep need for social connection and when that need is acute, like it is after the experience of exclusion, people adjust their behavior to increase the chance of connection. In this case, the need for social connection pushed people to agree with others, even though they had to give the wrong answer. They were willing to give up a bit of freedom for connection.

You've also almost certainly, knowingly or unknowingly, changed your interests or beliefs, maybe just a bit, to make a connection with a new acquaintance. Maybe you've expressed or exaggerated your interest in sports or politics, literature or wine, because you believed the other person liked these things.

I'm not talking about professing love for something you hate or
know nothing about; it's more like shading the truth rather than
lying. And there is a reasonable chance that you will come to
believe the views you express.[3]

The need for social connection affects behavior in both obvious and incredibly subtle ways that can elude our conscious
awareness. We change our behavior to smooth social interactions and make friends. Even the cadence of our voice and
body language changes. In one study, participants who walked
into a room and saw someone sitting in a dominant fashion—
leaning back, taking up lots of space—were more likely to sit
in a submissive way—hands in lap, body constricted, taking up
less space. When people walked into the room and encountered someone in a submissive posture, they were more likely
to take on a dominant one. Why does this happen? People want
to get along, and they intuitively understand that unlike other
aspects of social interaction where matching a partner's behavior increases liking, when it comes to power, complementing
the behavior of your partner leads to a smoother interaction.
This might seem counterintuitive, but imagine two people competing for the upper hand or two people waiting for the other
to take charge: these situations are less likely to go well than
when one person plays high and the other plays relatively low
status.[4,5,6]

Some might think they are immune to such shifting. But
those people are either wrong or without friends. Back in the
late 1990s, when I was in graduate school at the University of
California, Los Angeles, my colleagues and I conducted a study
in which people were led through a task by researchers wearing
a T-shirt that was either blank or read "Eracism." The T-shirt

was designed as a cue that the experimenter was against racism, as in erasing racism. The people were told the task was designed to measure reaction times to different objects, buildings, flowers, and words. In fact, the task we designed was to measure whether it was easier to associate Black rather than White faces with negative words.

In the task, Black or White faces were flashed on a screen so quickly that people didn't even know that faces had been shown at all. After each face, the word *good* or *bad* was displayed on the screen, and people were asked to press a key to identify which word they saw as quickly as they could. Typically, what we find in such tasks is that people are faster to identify the word *bad* than *good* following exposure to a Black face, and faster to identify the word *good* than *bad* following exposure to a White face.

When the researcher was wearing a blank T-shirt, people showed the typical pattern of response, but when the same researcher wore the "Eracism" T-shirt, the pattern went away. Keep in mind, the people in the study never reported that they saw any faces. What's going on here? The people in the study are shifting their associations with race toward what they think the researcher believes. Even this minimal interaction with a researcher appears to move people toward a shared reality. This suggests that what you think, possibly incredibly important beliefs, can move around simply as a matter of who you're with. To be friends with someone, to choose to interact with others, is to begin to agree with their views of the world. This work challenges the idea that your beliefs are simply your own. Who your friends are says a lot about who you are and will be.[7]

These little changes in what you say, the associations you

make, the way you present your self, and how you behave are all necessary parts of relationships. For a relationship to work you must create and exist in a shared reality. This often means making changes to fit with your friend or partner. Each of these changes is also a tiny limitation of your freedom, a constraint on what is possible. In these situations—as with the ball-tossing experiment—no one forces you to be one self or another, but the need and desire to connect demands it. When your behavior bends to your relationship needs you've accepted a limitation on freedom.[8]

The idea that you're constantly shifting, that something as slight as an interaction with a new person can affect your "true" self, might feel wrong. I know who I am, and presumably you feel similarly. I get it, but much of the time we probably don't even notice these small changes, and when we do notice that our thoughts or behaviors have shifted, we are as likely to believe we chose the changes as to know that the demands of relationships caused them. The truth is that our interactions with others are constantly shaping our selves, and in this sense imposing limits on what we are and can be.

But who cares if the way you talk shifts toward someone you want to get along with? Well, the idea that even little inter-actions can affect the way you behave, even if only temporarily, shows the power of relationships to constrain our behavior. And not all changes are fleeting.[9]

Consider an intense relationship you had when you were younger. For the sake of argument let's think about a romantic relationship. The relationship surely affected your self at the time: the way you saw your self, the way others saw you, the way you behaved were all affected by the relationship. Now let's assume that relationship ended. Whether it ended well or badly, whether you ended it or the other person did doesn't matter. The relationship changed you in a way that can't be taken back—time runs in one direction. Perhaps you're more sensitive to rejection than you were before, perhaps you're more emotionally available, which has affected future relationships, but whatever you're feeling now about the relationship, or even whether you think about it, that relationship altered what you could become. You cannot be a person who was never touched by that relationship.

For those of us who put a premium on freedom, the idea that relationships limit freedom sounds terrible. I think this is due to a particular understanding of constraint. The word *constraint* conjures images of small spaces and straitjackets. Rather than *constraint*, we should probably use the word *structure*. Relationships create structure. Think of it like the lines in a coloring book. You can't have a picture if you don't color in the lines, but there's plenty of room for expression within the lines. Relationships limit, but they also *create* the picture of your self.

The idea that you can do anything, be with anyone, *be* anyone might sound exciting, but without structure, without limits, such freedom would leave you untethered to the world. Without relationships, without constraint, how would you even know your self? Think about it. When you define your self you are describing limits that make you *you*. If you say you are a programmer, a parent, a singer or a swimmer, a woman or a man, you are marking your place in the world and your connections to other people. All your identities help people understand you and help *you* understand your self. To have freedom is to eliminate these limits, to have no boundaries, to escape the bonds that hold your world together. What are we to make of the world, what can this all mean if there is nothing holding it together, if it's all just a series of disconnected events? Freedom challenges the coherence, the very existence, of self.

The fact that structure is necessary doesn't mean we always want to embrace it. To understand your place in the world, if only temporarily, can be nice, but it's not something that we always want. Sometimes we chafe under a shared reality that defines us, and the relationships that create that reality. We've seen and heard these stories countless times: the high school student who dreams of becoming an artist but whose parents push them to become a doctor, lawyer, or engineer. The college kid who feels uncomfortable at a party friends dragged him to. The spouse who feels trapped in a marriage. Or maybe even the parent who feels their world closing in on them as the demands of parenting escalate. Sometimes we need freedom even if it means creating distance in relationships we value.

In the early 2000s, researchers in the psychology department and the Fuqua School of Business at Duke University set out to see if people would actively reject a relationship partner's goal for them. In their studies they asked participants to list people close to them who wanted them to either have more fun or work harder. The researchers also measured the extent to which the people thought these close others were controlling. When researchers had people think about a controlling person who wanted them to work harder, people performed less well on the task than when they thought about someone who wanted them to "have more fun." In other words, when people close to you try to control you, you might actively resist their influence. And, as we've seen, this probably means creating distance within the relationship.[10]

Whether structure is a source of comfort or pain, it's unavoidable. We need structure to make sense of the world in order to navigate every aspect of our lives. Sometimes we seek new worlds or to expand the world we occupy, but this freedom is not without cost. The world is a blooming, buzzing place, and we impose structure and accept limitations to make it livable.

Think of the most positive relationship you have. My guess is part of what makes the relationship great is that you like the version of the self you are in it. You feel your best in this relationship. Consider that self for a moment. How would you describe it or define it? To describe or define your best self is to accept limits, constraints on what you are. In this context, constraint should be a source of comfort, more a hug than a straitjacket.

AT THE START OF THIS chapter, I noted that people say they are willing to lay down their lives for the idea of freedom. In many of these examples it turns out that what people are willing to die for is a socially constructed idea. Patriots don't die for freedom; they die for their nation. It seems people are at least as willing to die for structure as for freedom.

Why is freedom such a powerful touchstone for some of us? Maybe because we have come to believe that being free is to be your true self. But now we know that's completely backward. To be free, a being unaffected by others, not bound by norms and customs, untethered to the current moment, is to be without self.

You cannot be completely free in any relationship, but you can't know or be your self without them. This leaves you with a stark choice, which really is no choice at all. If freedom entails infinite possibilities of being, you can't be completely free and have a self. Maybe then what we need and want isn't freedom as I've described it, so much as the *feeling* of being free.

# 5

## Building Selves

*Our friends, how seldom visited, how little known—it is true; and yet, when I meet an unknown person, and try to break off, here at this table, what I call "my life," it is not one life that I look back upon; I am not one person; I am many people; I do not altogether know who I am—Jinny, Susan, Neville, Rhoda, or Louis: or how to distinguish my life from theirs.*

—Virginia Woolf, *The Waves*

Did you wake up this morning and ask yourself, Am I "me" today? Did you do this yesterday? Will you tomorrow? I don't think I ever have. But maybe, if you are willing to ask the question, you might be willing to accept that other people are in there with you: you are a bit of your mother and best friend and romantic partner. It seems fine to accept that others affect the way you talk and dress, where you work, and the way you spend your leisure time, assuming you like these other people, of course. Although, when we start to notice we are "becoming our mother or father," it might not feel great.

Putting aside the potential horror of aging into your parents for a second, how do you know where the boundary between you and close others is? Maybe you have the experience of saying something and not knowing if it was you or your mother/father/partner speaking. I've certainly had thoughts and couldn't be sure if they were truly mine or something I had picked up from someone close to me or some other random source.

This isn't about knowing where I heard this or that fact. It's about expressing a belief or an opinion as if it's your own, and then wondering if it originated with you, if you can legitimately claim ownership. Were the thoughts you expressed yours or someone else's? Here's the trippy thing: The question if they are yours or someone else's misses the point. They could be yours *and* someone else's at the same time.

When you wake up in the morning and know it's you, what is it that you know? You probably know where you differ from close others. I might know I don't agree with my father's political beliefs. I might know that I disagree with my partner on how to school our children. We might share a lot in common with our close others, but we are clearly not the same selves. Faculty members often work very closely with the students, and it's not uncommon to see a professor's students start to take on some of their advisor's mannerisms. I've seen the way students speak, the way they pose questions shift toward their advisor's style. We all choose to be around people similar to us, and in small and large ways we become more similar to the people we are around. In very extreme cases it's possible that the overlap becomes so great that you can feel like you inhabit someone else. But mostly we know that we are not one and the same with anyone else. At the same time, it's a bit odd to define our unique self as what we are not. It could be that sometimes we don't realize that some aspect of our self is shared with others. And because we cannot see where our self overlaps with others, we think of it as our unique self.

If that's right, our sense of self depends on ignorance: we assume our selves exist in the absence of overlap with other selves. If I know that some mannerism of mine is something I picked up from a close friend, maybe I think of that as less *my* self than I would if I believed it arose from some inner source. In this view, I see my self when I look around and no one else is there. The self, here, is defined by absence, by empty space.

An affirmative way to define the self would be to identify overlapping aspects of our self. Rather than thinking in terms of a pure self, unadulterated by the influence of other relationships, maybe we should think in terms of unique overlaps. A little bit of this relationship and a little bit of that one is what makes us unique.

If the idea that much of your self is literally a mix of other selves makes you uncomfortable, you aren't alone. People sometimes use the language of "losing" your self in a relationship to describe this discomfort. You might be fine "losing" your self in a whirlwind romance. But many people recoil at the idea of a permanent loss of self in another, or having the self completely defined in terms of close others. Consider how, in the last chapter, we examined the reaction against the wishes of close others whom we view as controlling. This creates a bit of conundrum for close relationships. How do you bond closely with another without "losing" your self?

THERE ARE FEW THINGS IN life as important as close relationships. Family, friends, romantic partners, these relationships comfort and antagonize, drain and sustain us. The idea that relationships create selves is easiest to see when you think about close relationships. Who would you be, *what* would you be if sheared of relationships with family, close friends, or romantic partners?

We are exquisitely sensitive to close relationships. Early on we learn language, the correct way to behave, and imbibe important social beliefs from our family and friends. Close relationships are the conduit through which we learn what the world is and how to be human in it. What should people eat? What constitutes "polite" conversation? What groups of people matter and what don't? What even are the different "categories" of people? The social structure of our world, and our place in it, are created and communicated in relationships.

I've already used the term *close others*, without saying much about what makes someone close to us. What does it mean to be close to others if the self *is* interactions with others? Here, *close* means the extent to which the self is overlapping with some other self. The closer you are to someone, the more your two selves overlap, the harder it is to distinguish one self from another.[1,2,3] Think back to the enfacement effect. We are literally able to incorporate someone else's face into our experience of self. It's harder to imagine a clearer example of overlap than seeing a face composed more of someone else and thinking, That's (mostly) me!

The idea of overlap—being a part of someone else and being made up of others—might sound outlandish. That we humans are not separate entities connected to others by words and deeds but, instead, are overlapping intersections of relationships, probably doesn't match the way you typically feel. The only thing that makes this sound even plausible is the existence of close relationships. You've probably had the experience of a relationship that feels like it's a part of you. Sometimes people talk about the birth of their child this way. You might feel this way about your life partner, as if they exist inside you. To have the relationships severed would be to rip out a part of your self. You would, quite simply, be less *you* without them. Maybe you've been in relationships where you would sacrifice your life for the other person. What do such relationships tell us about selves?

The first conscious experience many of us have features our family. My first clear memory is from when I was three or four years old, walking the grounds of Singing River Hospital in Pascagoula, Mississippi, feeding ducks with my mom. For me that memory represents a sort of birth—I start the construction of my conscious self from that moment—but I wouldn't count that as the birth of my self. I also wouldn't say that my self was born three or so years earlier. People were constructing my self as soon as my parents started to anticipate my arrival. Before I was conceived, my parents had ideas of how they would be as parents, what they would do differently than their parents. Whether I would be a boy or girl and what that would mean. They were creating ideas of me that were shaping their sense of self. Stories were being told, creation myths constructed that would shape the relationships people would have with me, and therefore shape my self.

We don't come into a world of unlimited possibilities. We are all subject to the demands of our times. We come into the world with some part of our paths decided by culture and heritage. Our families, the people we grow up around, their privileges and disadvantages, their joys and pains, strengths and foibles, celebrations and squabbles all play a crucial role in who we are and what we will become.

THE FACT THAT MUCH OF reality is socially constructed, and that this construction happens at multiple levels—interpersonal, group, national—creates vulnerability. If your self is being created and the environment that that self inhabits is also constructed, you might find your self at odds with the world. For example, you might experience your self as independent— perhaps you were raised that way by your parents—but the world constructed around you forces you to engage as dependent on others more powerful than you—maybe you're a woman in a sexist society.

The ideas of gaslighting and crazy-making capture one danger of social construction particularly well. Our understanding of the term *gaslighting*, which we now use to mean purposefully making someone question their reality, comes from an Oscar-winning 1944 movie, *Gaslight*. In the movie, a young opera singer named Paula is swept into a whirlwind romance and quick marriage to a charming musician. Soon into their life together, strange things start happening. Paula loses a brooch that she thought was safely put away, a picture disappears from the wall, Paula hears footsteps in the attic, and the gaslights in the house get dimmer and then brighter for no reason. Her husband convinces Paula that the flickering light and footsteps are in her imagination and that she is actually the one who took the missing things. Paula becomes increasingly isolated and comes to believe that she's a kleptomaniac, even though she doesn't remember taking any of the things, including her husband's watch, which he tells her she's taken. After several incidents, Paula truly believes she's going crazy and vows to not go out in public. It turns out, of course, that her husband is the cause of the flickering lights, footsteps, and missing items and he's been lying to make Paula think she is insane. He immersed Paula in a world that challenged her existing beliefs, many of them about herself. But her self permanently changed by existing in this relationship.

In what we might call crazy-making, you are forced to inhabit a world in which your basic assumptions about your self are at odds with the dominant cultural narrative. If you're a woman or an ethnic minority, people might casually assume you are incompetent, even in domains where you know you excel. In Eileen Pollack's *The Only Woman in the Room*, she describes her experience as one of Yale's first two women to earn a bachelor of science in physics in the 1970s. Although Pollack excelled in her classes, she felt isolated and dealt with almost daily microaggressions from classmates and faculty. Her peers insinuated that she was only given the opportunity to earn a physics degree because the university was attempting to fulfill affirmative action quotas. When she asked a classmate for homework help in her freshman year, he told her that she "had no intuitive feel for science." He then said, "Don't worry, Eileen. When I'm a big professor, you can be my assistant and run my lab." Even the facilities implied that women didn't belong. When she was taking math classes necessary for her physics degree, Pollack remembers having to climb to the top floor of the mathematics building to use the restroom because it was the only women's bathroom there.

She vividly remembers the switch in encouragement and praise she felt when taking her first writing class after years of physics classes in which she felt discouraged and alone. Ultimately, Pollack abandoned her dream to become a theoretical physicist. She became an author instead. In her book, Pollack interviewed many other women who earned or tried to earn STEM degrees and discovered that even though there was usually more than one woman in the room when her book was published in 2015, the feeling that women don't belong or have to work twice as hard to prove themselves capable still existed.[4]

What happens when it seems like the world is organized around this belief of incompetence? What happens when, as in Eileen's story, the belief is so ingrained that people deny that it even exists? Whether others purposefully manipulate your sense of reality or "just" accept and defend beliefs and social structures that devalue people like you, living in a world that violates your reality can challenge your sense of sanity.

CLOSE RELATIONSHIPS COLLECT, MAGNIFY, AND inject much of what's happening in the world into the most intimate areas of our lives. Big societal changes that can often feel abstract—like the shifts in the economy and high-level cultural changes—constantly brush against us in our day-to-day comings and goings: fellow public transit riders too engrossed in phones for a nod of recognition, low-paid grocery store clerks irritated by a question we ask, the happy person who held the door for you, the kind person who picked up that pen you dropped. These interactions leave marks on us. We arrive at home refreshed from pleasant interactions, or tired and aggravated by the rudeness of small slights accumulated during the day. Our day-to-day interactions, in other words, become part of the self we bring to our close relationships.

By bringing their external interactions into our relationships, close relationship partners expand us. This can add to their charm, the way they nourish us with experiences beyond those we have on our own. But you can love people and want to maintain a certain kind of distance from them. Maybe there is something uncomfortable about what they bring to your interactions, or the pressure they exert on your self. Maybe their political views conflict with your sense of morality. Maybe you worry that the strength of their personality or confidence will overwhelm your sense of self. Maybe the way they see you is not the way others do, or the way you would like to see yourself. In these situations, you might still want the relationship, but also want to protect your self from unwanted feelings and influences. In these situations, the relationships might change you, the relationships might begin to wither, or you might actively resist their demands of you.[5]

Dissatisfaction in a relationship is often the result of conflicting ideas about your "self" that arise from other relationships in your life. If you are completely defined in one relationship, where would conflict come from? Imagine all you ever knew was who you are in relationship to your mother. If your mother completely defined you and you completely defined her, where would tension arise? Cult leaders understand this well. When you're cut off from family and friends, the reservoir from which challenges would flow is drained, the version of you that might resist certain beliefs withers. But it's almost impossible to be completely defined in any one relationship or even any one community. That our selves are defined by multiple relationships creates the possibility for conflict. Who we are in one relationship or community might not sit well with who we are in another.

Imagine someone in their first serious romantic relationship. Up until that point the most important relationships, the most defining relationships in the person's life were likely close friends or family. The new relationship will almost certainly create changes to the person's self. These changes could come into conflict with the self that friends and family had come to know. When relationships construct conflicting views of self (self in romantic relationships conflicts with self in parental relationships), you might experience it as a conflict between you and a close other (say your parent).

Close relationships are complicated. We've probably all had relationships that weren't the best, but that we either didn't want to or felt like we couldn't leave. It's particularly tough when these relationships are with people close to us. How do you manage a fraught relationship with the people who matter the most? If you define your self as a child of your parents, what happens to that part of your self when you diminish or try to exit that relationship? How might it shift your childhood memories, how might it shift your self? To completely protect your self from a relationship might require you to give up the part of your self created in that relationship by ending it.

Perhaps we must let go of the idea that you can simply decide not to be affected by close others. The idea that you have control of some core of your self and can shield it from the effects of your relationships is flawed. What you do have is a complex array of relationships that make up the self. Rather than trying to erect a barrier within problematic relationships, you might be able to augment the effect of others. Perhaps the best way to mute the effect of a relationship, short of ending it, is to increase the time you spend on other relationships or in unrelated communities. If you don't like the influence of, say, your parents, spending more time with friends or romantic partners might blunt the effect that your parents have, *but* doing so might, actually it almost certainly will, create a degree of distance that ultimately undermines the parental relationship.

PEOPLE NEED AND ENJOY THE experience of being close to other people. We seem hard-wired to connect with others, especially those who we believe to be like us. If you continue to interact with others, over time your attitudes and beliefs tend to converge. This shared experience of the world can be quite comforting. You feel like the world makes sense, and you see it clearly, but the idea that your experience of the world is dependent on others calls into question your freedom. Freedom wouldn't mean very much if others dictated the parameters of what is possible. And yet, without close others our sense of reality would be impaired.

We often behave as if reality is a given; it's just out there and we see it, and presumably so does everyone else. But much of what we take for reality is not just "how it is"; it is constructed with others.[6] For example, imagine you are asked to estimate the distance that a point of light on the other side of a dark room is moving. This task is something that most people have little experience with or prior knowledge about, and so your response is just a guess. You would have no way of judging the accuracy of this guess; however, when placed in a group, you have far more information available to you. You are likely to listen to what your group members have to say and adjust your estimate accordingly. In reality, the movement of the light is merely an optical illusion. What is objectively true of the world is irrelevant in this case. What matters are the people around us. We adjust our estimates based on what others say, because we see this information as valuable and useful for making sense of our world.[7]

Surely you've been in situations where you didn't understand what was happening. Maybe you saw someone walking ahead of you collapse. Or maybe you encountered a large group of angry people shouting in front of an office building. If you're like most people, which you most assuredly are if you're human, you probably looked around to see how others were responding. You use those other people to try to decide if you should offer help to the person who collapsed or if you should be afraid of an angry mob or support a righteous protest. That's what humans do: we lean on each other to make sense of the world around us.

Much of what we take for granted as reality has already been given to us by our relationships and communities. Early familial relationships shape our tastes and attitudes, friends teach us acceptable behaviors, romantic partners teach us something about intimacy. We learn through social interactions. We learn the way of the world through mundane and complex interactions with those closest to us. These relationships create a riot of color and forms that we experience as the world.[8]

It's incredible, really, that in an unfathomably complex world, we experience a sense of "seeing" and understanding it, that we engage with the world (more or less) effectively. We owe much of this to our close relationships. Close others help us make sense of the world—the world makes sense when it makes sense to "us." We spin worlds around and out of our relationships.

Look around at your life and think about the people in it. Now imagine a completely different set of people. How much would your life change? You can probably see plenty of changes. Maybe you'd eat different food, have a different job, spend more time outdoors and less time shopping or vice versa. You might become a clean freak or a slob. And what you can imagine almost certainly is only a small fraction of the way the world would change for you. As far as you would be concerned, the world, your reality, would shift into something new.

This is the power of self as constructed in relationships: it reflects, projects, and creates worlds, based on the social realities that exist around it.

WE'VE FOCUSED ON WHAT IT means to have a self, but there is also the question of how we know the self. The idea of a self as a set of relationships might be hard to grasp or accept, but the idea of knowing the self through relationships is a bit easier.

We often talk of our selves and others in absolute terms. We say someone is short or tall, fat or skinny, athletic or clumsy as if these things mean something by themselves. What we mean is that they are fatter than some ideal, or more or less athletic than those we know. We make sense of each other and our selves in comparison to others. Often the "others" is really an understanding of an average or some unstated norm (e.g., over six feet is tall), but there is still some social comparison.

If a self is composed of relationships and interactions, then close relationships should be a significant part of our selves. Not only do you spend considerable time with your close others, but you also make sense of the world with them. You share your joys and fears. They are your fellow travelers through life. When you are with these people it can feel as if you are your "true" self.

At the same time, people close to you can be your biggest competitors, your bête noir, a nemesis, the thorn forever in your side. Even these people might reveal something true about your self—you just might not want to see it.[9,10]

Close relationships, in playing an outsize role in defining us, also place greater constraints on what we can be than more fleeting interactions or relationships. The more you overlap with someone, the more their view of the world becomes your view. Imagine you have a close sibling. It could be that their view of romantic relationships shapes, in part, your view of relationships. If their view changes it could influence the quality of your relationships.

If you choose your close relationship, the desire to maintain a coherent view of your self can cause you to believe you must desire, or at least embrace, the consequences of that relationship choice. If you pined for a child, and then you have one, you might downplay the sleep deprivation and other costs of parenthood to make sense of your choice, and probably to maintain your sanity. If you feel like you had a choice in a certain relationship, you are motivated to downplay the costs associated with your choice. When there is a tension between a choice you've made and your experience of the consequences of that choice, you shift your experience of the consequences to better align with the fact that you (knowingly) brought them on your self.[11]

Sometimes a relationship can feel claustrophobic—suddenly you find yourself in interactions that you can't avoid, ones that always end in a frustrating argument, or leave you feeling lesser than or disgusted by the person's weakness. Maybe it's a marriage coming apart at the seams because your ambitions are not aligned. Maybe it's a friendship where you no longer see situations the same, and you no longer get the support you need for your view of your life's struggles. Whatever the reason, the connection to them—the inclusion of their self in yours—pushes your buttons. If you've been in such situations, you probably know the frustration, fear, or anger that they can produce. In these situations, there's a feeling of limitation. You can't be the person you would like to be. The relationship is holding you back in some way. The other person's choices, their behaviors, their way of being in you are impinging on you.

But, in many such situations—though not all—you *choose* to interact with the person. I don't want to overstate this. There are situations where power is at play. Maybe you depend on the person financially; maybe your ability to maintain other relationships you value depends on maintaining one you don't. But for some reason the cost of remaining in the relationship outweighs the cost of severing ties.

The cost to the self of severing a tie tells another story about tough relationships. The idea that the cost is an external impingement can't be quite right. Some of what happens in tough relationships emanates from *your* self. Of course, it takes two to tango, but I'm talking about the fact that the close other is a part of you, and what bothers you about them is likely a part of you, too.

To loathe a close other is to loathe a part of the self. We wouldn't be who we are without them being what they are. Maybe the trouble in close relationships comes from our feelings about the other person, but perhaps also from our feelings regarding ourselves.

# 6
---

# I Am Because We Are

*Umuntu ngumuntu ngabantu.*

—Zulu phrase translated as
"I am because we are."

Close relationships ground us. There is a physicality in these relationships; we see and touch these people. We know family and close friends, and some enemies, directly, viscerally. The mere presence of some family members can cause joy or pain. People can speak of a room smelling of their partner, the look of their partner's stride, and the feel of their hug. For others, perhaps a certain perfume or cologne triggers memories of a neglectful or abusive parent. In Christina Crawford's telling of her abusive childhood, *Mommie Dearest*, she recounts that seeing wire clothes hangers in her closet would send her mother, the actress Joan Crawford, into a rage. Joan's mother, Christina's grandmother, worked for years in a dry cleaners and Christina muses that wire hangers reminded her mother of her former poverty. In an iconic, and frequently memed, scene in the movie version, Joan drags her young daughter out of bed and beats her with a wire hanger while shouting "No more wire hangers!"

For better or worse, we know these people so intimately because they shape our experience of the world. They play a large part in defining who we are. It's easy to understand the power of these kinds of relationships, but these kinds of close relationships aren't the only relationships that define us. We are members of ethnic groups, citizens of nations, fans of teams, alumni of universities. Relationships with these groups define us.[1,2,3]

The social worlds we inhabit are unbelievably complex. Groups help tame this complexity. When I meet someone new, I'm not meeting a unique individual I know nothing about. I'm meeting a member of a multitude of groups I already know. Let's say you're at a bar sitting next to someone. Whether the person is a man or woman, is a member of your racial group or not, seems old or young, rich or poor will almost certainly affect the way you interact with the person. In fact, your perception of their group memberships is likely to affect whether you have a conversation at all.

Social identities are tied to or drive some of the most intractable social problems we face today, like economic inequality, racism, sexism, political polarization, and xenophobia, to name a few.[4,5] Some people—often members of powerful groups, for reasons we will explore—suggest that we can address these problems by simply ignoring or denying the importance of social identities. Supreme Court justice John Roberts wrote, "The way to stop racial discrimination is to stop discriminating on the basis of race."[6] While it's possible that race as we currently understand it could cease to influence our social lives, the idea that discrimination based on social group membership will go away is a pipe dream. The complexity of the world, the need for social structure, the basic human desire to be a part of a group means that we gravitate toward people we see as similar to us and engage with others based on our perception of their group memberships.[7]

Imagine a world without social identities—no gender, race, nationality, class, sports fandom, professional affiliations, or alma maters, etc. It might or might not be a better place, but it would certainly be more difficult to navigate. When you meet new people, whether you know it or not, you think you know quite a lot about them. Why? Because you have some sense of groups they belong to. They look to be men or women, young or old, Black, White, Asian, or Latino, rich or poor. Maybe they dress like preppies or hipsters, or wear swag from their university or place of work. All of this tells you something about them. These identities give us a foundation from which to grow or decide to not grow a relationship. Without the shortcuts social groups provide, you'd have to build an understanding for every person you interact with from scratch.

Relationships with social groups help us understand where we belong and provide a sense of the way the world works. My gender, race, and profession help me understand what's expected of me and what I can expect from others—whether I like or agree with it or not. For me this means that people have often been surprised by my profession, and that the respect I've been accorded varies greatly depending on whether people know my profession. When I was just starting out as a professor in my late twenties, people just wouldn't believe it when I told them my job. It's true I was young, which was also a social identity at odds with expectations of my profession, but I doubt many of my fellow young colleagues who happened to be White experienced some of what I did. People accused me of making it up when I told them I was a professor at Stanford. Someone—not a security guard, mind you, just someone in the building—asked me for my ID on my way to my office. A student approached my (White) advisee assuming he must be the professor rather than me. A PhD student told me that her advisor told her she might not want to work with me because I might be an "affirmative action" hire. I've also, on the other side, been spared some of the sexist behavior my female colleagues must manage. I haven't had the experience of someone trying to undermine my authority because of my gender. These experiences show me what others expect based on my identities, and I've learned to manage these expectations. The view from these and other identities gives me an understanding of what to expect in my life and how to navigate the world.[8,9]

But these groups didn't show up out of nowhere. We didn't discover them—we created them. Yes, differences in things like skin tone and hair texture and color exist in nature, but meaningful social groups tied to these differences are social creations. We create social groups and we also change them when it suits those in power. The boundaries of empires and nations shift and the people who count in the category of subjects and citizens shift with them. But even though we create them, we treat social groups as if they represent some eternal truth about the people in them, as if members have some unseen essence that explains the stories we tell about their groups.[10,11]

Think about how many stories we hear that revolve around the idea of some innate worth hidden by circumstance of birth—a noble child hidden from an enemy or accidentally switched at birth—that inevitably reveals itself as the true nature of the "chosen one" emerges. In many of the stories we tell, lineage just destines some for greatness. This is the tale of Moses in the scriptures, Luke Skywalker in *Star Wars*, Harry Potter, Jon Snow in *Game of Thrones*. These are stories we tell to make sense of the world we live in, to justify the differences we see.

We tell stories about people and groups, and then behave as if the story reflects the truth of the group. The truth is that it's the other way around—the story created the group. Let's say I see a group of people who share some trait; in this case let's say they were born east of a river I live beside. These east siders seem lazy—they don't work as hard as we do, or as hard as we think people should. Whatever the case, I label them all as part of a group, and say that whatever makes east siders east siders causes them to be lazy. Then I expect all people east of the river to share this trait, because whatever makes someone an east sider also causes laziness.

In this little example, there were no east siders until a story was told about people who shared a physical space. The story was an attempt to make sense of a difference I saw between a group of "not my" people and the people I live among. Maybe people on the east side of the river don't even think of themselves as a group. Also, my sense that they are lazy is relative to the way my people behave or my people's beliefs about how people should behave. The story I told created the group and fit their existence within my worldview. This story also affirms my group as hardworking and suggests how I should think about and interact with east siders.

Social groups and identities are a neat trick. The "trick" is the creation of a social reality from thin air, a layer we've painted atop the world. We engage social groups as if they have a meaning other than the ones we give them, as if a social group is a thing like a stone or a tree, a thing that can exist without us.[12,13]

We create social groups, at least in part, *because* they do work. We use social groups to make sense of the world, to justify or challenge the way things are, to understand our place in the world and to imagine other possibilities, to know who we are and who we can be. The social world is complicated. People are motivated by wants and needs, fears and insecurities that they sometimes don't even understand. And people often aren't aware of the ways their behavior affects those around them. This is the world we are all trying to manage. A world in which you try to assess the motivations of others, to parse the meaning of their behaviors, all in service of understanding the best way to engage with them given your sometimes sketchy understanding of your own motivations. To negotiate these complexities one person at a time can be overwhelming, so we simplify. The existence of social groups allows us to treat individuals as members of categories that we can make sense of, rather than as a vast number of unique individuals.

We know our selves and others through relationships to groups. When we identify with a group, it creates a boundary that helps define us. When I identify as a man, I understand features of myself through the lens offered by manhood. As a simple example, if someone refers to me as "big" I don't take it as an insult. Larger size is associated with more dominance and men are supposed to be dominant, so being "big" is generally a good thing, and I understand it as such. Most women I know wouldn't take kindly to being called "big." Because I know that physical size is understood through the lens of gender, I wouldn't use *big* to describe the way my female friends look. That I know a friend identifies as a woman makes it easier for me to interact with her effectively. Rather than dealing with each person as a unique instance of a human being, my knowledge of gender allows me to make certain assumptions that simplify my dealings with others.

Social identities take us beyond the immediate, intimate connections we have with the people we see every day. Today, for example, to be a member of a nation is to be connected to millions or billions of people. To be a member of a nation is to be connected to the past and the future of your nation. This is true of all social identities: they extend us. Social identities are time machines: they connect us to a history that preceded our birth and allow us to imagine our place in a future past our physical deaths.

In his powerful exploration of the history of slavery, *Slavery and Social Death: A Comparative History*, Orlando Patterson, a professor of sociology, wrote, "Slaves differed from other human beings in that they were not allowed freely to integrate the experiences of their ancestors into their lives, to inform their understanding of social reality with the inherited meanings of their natural forebears, or to anchor the living present in any conscious community of memory." To be without a social past, to be without ancestral ties, is to not exist as fully human. It is to be socially dead. For Patterson, "the essence of slavery is that the slave, in his social death, lives on the margin between community and chaos, life and death."[14]

Social identities don't just give us existential weight by placing us in time; they also expand us. If you feel pride or shame in the founding of your nation; if you feel anger when reflecting on wrongs done to your ancestors; if you hope for the success of your alma mater's sports teams, you understand what I mean by expansion. The behavior of those who preceded you and the accomplishments yet to be made by those who will follow you become your own. In the grand scheme of things our individual lives are small, but social identities allow us to transcend these limits.

You cannot have a social identity without a social group; social identities are created by ties among people and the mutual recognition of these ties. Who these people are, what they do, becomes part of you. Across a number of studies I've worked on, people focused on their *group*'s advantages to emphasize their *personal* work ethic, report having had a tougher life, and support for policies that they perceive to harm their group, presumably to even the scales. When you are a part of a group, their pain is your pain, their shame is your shame, their guilt is your guilt. This is one cost of the expansion, the personal transcendence offered by social identity.[15,16,17,18,19]

IN HIS BOOK *WHITE BY Law: The Legal Construction of Race*, Ian Haney López describes a case decided by a federal court in California in 1878. The case was brought by a Chinese national, Ah Yup. At the time only free Whites and people of African descent could become citizens of the United States. Ah Yup was suing to have Chinese people classified as White. Specifically, the question in the case *In re Ah Yup* was "Is a person of the Mongolian race a 'white Person?'" After significant consideration of anthropological writings on racial science, advice from members of the bar, and a close reading of the legislative history on who counted as White, the judge decided "that a native of China, of the Mongolian race, is not a white person." Based on that conclusion, and the law regarding naturalization, Ah Yup was denied citizenship in the United States.

Race, with its presumed biological basis and clear social importance, provides a great example of the complexity involved in the construction of social identity. In *White by Law*, we see both state and federal courts struggle to determine who does and does not count as White in the United States. Through the history that López lays out, you can see the concept of race being defined and refined over time. You can also see the effort necessary to maintain boundaries that form the racial hierarchy in the United States. The connection between race and citizenship also demonstrates the way the creation of one identity can affect others. For example, the Immigration Act of 1924 was designed to minimize immigration from areas other than western and northern Europe. If to be American is to be White, protection of America requires protection of Whiteness. The need to maintain boundaries requires work and vigilance, because race is not a self-evident or objective feature of people.[20,21,22]

It's worth pointing out the obvious: in the case of race, variation in skin tones slides rather than leaps from alabaster to obsidian, and the same is true of just about every other physical characteristic people tie to race. For instance, I consider myself Black and most people in the United States immediately see me as Black. Now, not many people in West Africa, where my African ancestry likely originated, would look at me and assume I am West African. Like most African Americans I have a mixture of European and African ancestry. In the United States, there is a history of applying a "one-drop" rule for the purpose of maintaining hereditary slavery and racial segregation after that. Any African ancestry was enough to categorize someone as Black. In some Caribbean and South American nations, however, race varies along a continuum of physical appearance.[23] This difference allows the possibility that a person could wake up White in one place, take a flight, and be Black a few hours later.

These ways of thinking about race continue to affect people's lives. In 2011, actress Halle Berry, a South African by birth and by media accounts the daughter of a White mother and Black father, was fighting for custody of her two-year-old daughter against her former husband, a White man. The question of their daughter's race became part of the argument after Berry accused her husband of using derisive racial terms and refusing to see their daughter as biracial. During an interview for *Ebony* magazine, the actress said, "I feel she's Black. I'm Black and I'm her mother, and I believe in the one-drop theory."[24]

Despite the creation of race as a social category, we talk as if racial groups reflect a clear (biological) divide between people. Paradoxically, the talk about "mixed" people, people who claim parents from different racial groups, demonstrates the absurdity of the situation and the confusion it creates. The use of the term *mixed* implies that other people somehow *aren't* mixed, that such people are "pure."

Sometimes people will say they use the term *mixed* to capture a mixed cultural heritage, rather than a biological one. People who have been immersed in two different cultural backgrounds and worldviews could be considered mixed. But does this truly capture the way people respond to the complexities of racial boundaries?

• • •

In 2015, Rachel Dolezal, then president of the Spokane, Washington, chapter of the National Association for the Advancement of Colored People (NAACP), resigned after it was revealed both her parents were White. I say revealed because Rachel had been living as a Black woman, which most people understood to mean that at least one of her parents was Black. Rachel, despite her parents' race, identified as Black, both personally and publicly. When asked why she walked away when an interviewer inquired whether she was African American she said, "Yes, my biological parents were both white, but, after a lifetime spent developing my true identity, I knew that nothing about whiteness described who I was. At the same time, I felt it would have been an oversimplification to have simply said yes. After all, I didn't identify as African American; I identified as Black."[25]

Dolezal understood that the choice to identify as Black could have serious consequences. In her own words, "White folk would see you as a traitor and a liar and never trust you again, and Black folk might see you as an infiltrator and an imposter and never trust you again." Yet she chose to identify as Black anyway. We can't know for sure what drove Rachel to identify as she did, and in fact she might not have direct access to why, but we do know that it elicited negative responses from some Black folks.[26]

Why did people care and what does it tell us about group boundaries? One answer is that people thought Rachel lied about her race. For many in this camp, being Black requires having Black ancestry. Often this way of thinking defines race genetically; your racial identity is simply a matter of your genetic makeup. Race is not about the way you look; genes confer

the essence of Blackness. Physical features are mere manifesta-
tions of Blackness, not the thing itself. Even if you don't adopt
a genetic view of race, you might also be angry because you see
a deeply problematic asymmetry in someone like Rachel trying
to claim Blackness whereas those seen as Black can't legitimately
claim Whiteness.[27,28]

WHO WE THINK OF AS members of our group or not says something about what we think of our selves, who we think we are,
and what defines us. Imagine a machine that changes everything about a person's appearance from Black to White as they
walk through. Is the person who comes out Black or White?
Racial essentialists, those who believe that race is tied to some
unseen, unchangeable, inborn essence, would say that the person is still Black. Even if physical changes reflected genetic
changes, essentialists would still likely see the person as Black.
To become White requires becoming a different person entirely, not a different version of who you were. For an essentialist, the body is something that a self wears. The self is Black or
White; the body is just an outward manifestation of an internal,
unseen truth.

I would say it's a trick question. Whether you are Black or
White depends on the beliefs held in your relationships. Your
appearance only matters because it affects your relationships. In
America there are people who are considered Black by typical
standards—their parents would be categorized as Black—but
who look White enough that others believe they are White in
various contexts. If they are living among White people and
are seen as White by other Whites they are said to be "passing."

The first Black woman to get a degree from Vassar College

graduated more than forty years before Vassar started admitting African-American students.[29] Although Anita Hemmings had two "mulatto" parents (with both Black and White heritage), a Boston newspaper at the time reported that "she could pass anywhere simply as a pronounced brunette of white race." Anita applied for Vassar's class of 1897 as a White woman and was believed to be so until a few days before her graduation, when a suspicious roommate discovered her parents' race and outed her. In her later years, Anita married a Black doctor who also passed and the couple moved to Manhattan to live as White people. We have categories that are labeled by color and determined by physical appearance, but a "Black" person can still *appear* to be White and be afforded the benefits associated with Whiteness. This is racial essentialism at work.

The 2017 horror film *Get Out* captured the essential view of race perfectly. In the movie a White family discovers a way to transfer one person's being or consciousness into another person's body. This family, as does much of America, fetishizes Black bodies—their presumed innate athleticism, heightened sexuality, imperviousness to pain, etc.[30,31,32] And so they make a business of abducting Black people to auction them off as new physical vessels for older or less-able-bodied, wealthy White people. This concept works for a variety of reasons. It's easy to understand bodies as vessels because we believe the self is a thing inside the body. It's easy to imagine the selling of Black bodies for White consumption, because we understand the history of slavery and the continued status differential between Blacks and Whites. But perhaps most importantly, the concept of the movie depends on an acceptance of racial essentialism.

We get *Get Out* because we are practiced at essentialist

thinking. Children as young as four years old understand essential properties of groups. For example, if told a baby kangaroo is sent to live with a family of goats, children will predict that the kangaroo will be better at hopping than climbing, even if the kangaroo is too young to hop when it was adopted by the goats. The children have a sense that something they can't see makes a kangaroo a kangaroo and not a goat. They believe that this thing, this essence, defines the group and that outward appearances are caused by this essence.[33]

The belief that a thing's underlying nature, its essence, the unobservable thing that makes it what it is, causes its observable characteristics like size and color, taste and smell, preferences and talents is usually helpful. Kids are right that a kangaroo is going to hop no matter who raises it, or where it grows up. If you're foraging for mushrooms, it would be good to know that certain mushrooms are likely to be poisonous regardless of where you find them, or that certain *kinds* of mushrooms are poisonous. The belief in essences allows us to generalize beyond single examples, to kinds of things. But this can also cause confusion; we can mistake categories we create for natural categories we discover.[34]

Essentialist thinking is of course not limited to the way Americans think about race. Imagine you were born in Germany to German parents, but at birth you were adopted by a Swiss family and immediately taken to Switzerland. You grew up in Switzerland with no knowledge that you were born in Germany nor that your biological parents are German. Are you Swiss or German? We could treat the question as a legal one—are you eligible for Swiss or German citizenship?—and go look up the answer, but I am asking a more fundamental question. I am asking how we define membership in national groups. In this case, two characteristics could make you German: your biological parents are German and you were born in Germany. But your relationships would make you Swiss: you believe you are Swiss and so do the people you interact with.

If you think of nationality as defined by a biological essence tied to parentage, our adopted child is German. An essentialist might argue that there is something about "German genes" that makes you German. From this perspective, being German is like being someone's genetic offspring; it's a biological reality, not a social one—German-ness is an essence passed biologically. Kangaroos hop and goats climb no matter who raises them or where they grow up.

During the 2018 Winter Olympics, a commercial for AncestryDNA featured a young woman figure skating.[35] The voice-over went something like this: *Greatness lives in all of us . . . now is the time to discover yours. You can find out where you get your precision, your grace, your drive.* With "precision" a pie chart was superimposed over the skating woman, showing a percentage of Scandinavian heritage, with "grace" Central Asia, and with "drive" Great Britain. The ad suggested that the woman's ability was the result of her ancestry. It wasn't so crass to suggest that her inherited physical build drove her ability; you wouldn't need a genetic test for that. No, the clear suggestion was that more intangible characteristics—grace, precision, drive—coincide with the geographic location of your ancestry, a reality presumably written in your genetic code.

The mapping of the human genome, which allowed for the development of mass market genetic tests, is one of the most important scientific breakthroughs of the last century. But there is nothing novel about the use of science to suggest there are biological (often read as natural and immutable) differences between groups of people. During the heyday of racial science, roughly the seventeenth through the early twentieth centuries, there was a search for physical differences to justify the racial hierarchy.[36] This history, echoed in the ad for genetic testing, depends on the flexibility of essentialist thinking to make sense of our ever-shifting social realities.

As an example, for much of US history, ancestry from East Asia would not have been associated with grace. The Yellow Peril, *coolie*, and other derogatory labels tied to people of Asian descent were common when Asian immigrants were hired as cheap labor. As Asian Americans began to serve as a counterpoint to other ethnic minorities, primarily Black folks, and Asian countries helped the United States during the Cold War, characteristics tied to the essence of Asian-ness shifted. Rather than the former denigrating stereotype as primitive, shifty hordes from Asia, we now have the putatively positive (but still potentially harmful) stereotype of the mathematically gifted, graceful, but socially awkward Asian American.[37]

In contrast to the idea that social identities such as race denote some eternal characteristic of group members, humans have easily allowed their understanding of groups to shift as needed. For example, the underlying essence of Asian-ness has shifted to explain and justify the current social reality. Today your group is an un-American interloper; tomorrow it might be the new model minority. Magic! And Asian-ness isn't the only social identity that has shifted over time. Women have gone from being seen by men as sexually insatiable to today being seen as less interested in sex than men. Many descriptions of

African slaves focused on their childlike, docile natures, whereas today African Americans are more likely to be stereotyped as precociously dangerous.[38,39,40,41]

MANY SAW RACHEL DOLEZAL AS a White woman pretending to be Black, which aroused anger. People were upset by the asymmetry of a White person becoming Black, and the impossibility of the reverse. People were upset that by working on issues that affect Black people, her mendacity set their cause back. The idea that a White woman could appropriate a Black identity was compared to White people putting on blackface in minstrel shows.

We can never know what was really going on in Rachel's head, but let's assume that she was committed to her Black identity. The local community of Black people embraced her, until the truth of her racial identity came out. Black folks treated her as a full-fledged member of the Black community. She even attained a position of leadership in the local chapter of the NAACP. In fact, given her commitment to the identity, she might have experienced discrimination commonly directed toward Black women.

When Rachel decided she was a Black woman, she tacitly made claims about social groups and identity. She denied the idea that social identity, at least racial identity, is rooted in ancestry. To describe her racial identity she wrote, "Yes, my parents weren't Black, but that's hardly the only way to define Blackness. The culture you gravitate toward and the worldview you adopt play equally large roles. As soon as I was able to make my exodus from the white world in which I was raised, I made a headlong dash toward the Black one, and in the process

I gained enough personal agency to feel confident in defining myself that way." As she sees it, racial identity is, or at least can be, a choice.[42]

For Rachel, to be a member of a racial group is simply to choose to adopt a culture and a worldview. But this route to racial group membership seems inadequate, even for her. In addition to adopting the culture and worldview, Rachel cultivated a look that led people to assume she was Black and interact with her as such. Accordingly, her relationships were predicated on her identity as a Black woman; this was her ticket into the group. She could live as a Black woman because people accepted her as Black. Being Black is a *social* identity; you cannot be Black by yourself. Your ability to be Black, or any other social identity, depends on others sharing your view of yourself.

The idea that racial identity is a choice seemed to drive much of the antipathy toward Rachel. If the essence of being Black is genetic and we believe that genes are the basis of who we are, Blackness is written in your very being; Blackness is immutable. To suggest that racial identity is a choice challenges its immutability. Perhaps this creates a sense of unease. Mutability allows instability, which might be profoundly disconcerting if our sense of self relies on the feeling that our identities are stable. Social groups organize relationships; instability in our ties to social groups suggests instability in relationships. It's easy to see why such claims might raise someone's ire. Among people who define their selves by inclusion in these groups, to protect the integrity of the group boundary is to protect the self.[43]

Even if people don't define racial groups genetically, they might still care about heritage. If you are bound to your parents and ancestors as much socially as genetically, the idea of choice is still problematic. You can't choose your racial group any more than you can choose your parents and your heritage.

Maybe heritage isn't the issue, but the way others perceive and treat you determines racial group membership. Here a demand for stability might mean that those who have a choice to be perceived as something other than Black aren't *really* Black.

Social groups are defined collectively, but the definitions are often fuzzy. What if Rachel had been raised by Black parents, but a genetic test suggested she was only one-eighth Black? What if she was one-eighth Black, but was raised by White parents? What if she was raised by White parents, but after learning she was one-eighth Black she immersed herself in Black spaces and culture? What if she was raised by Black parents, looked Black, immersed herself in Black culture, but discovered she had no Black ancestry? In which of these situations, if any, is Rachel Black?

Social group definitions can take on a "I know it when I see it" flavor—ask, and a person might not be able to name the group boundaries, but they "just know" if someone belongs or not. You need information to decide people's group membership. You might want to know something about their parents' identities, where they were born, where they grew up, the circumstances of their youth. In a sense people need to submit a resume for membership in a social group. In most cases, with the right information, it's easy to determine who belongs in the group, but there is room for interpretation.

Sometimes when I travel abroad people ask me where I'm from. If I say I'm from the United States, they might ask where my parents are from. The implication is that at some point a family member was *not* from the United States; they want me to trace my heritage all the way back to the source, whatever that means, with this question. We all do some version of this. We want to understand what groups people belong to. It tells us who we are—or should be—when we are with them. It helps us understand how to interact with them. Sometimes a person's appearance is sufficient to place them, but in other cases we need more information. I need enough information about you to determine where you belong.

This idea of a resume highlights an important aspect of essentialist thinking. You can't directly see an essence—because no such thing exists for social groups—so group membership must be divined from imperfect markers. People are members of groups when the relevant people accept them as members of the group. This is what it looks like to have relationships dictate group membership.

Maybe people were mad at Rachel because they believed she lied on her application, that she was admitted to the group under false pretenses. She tricked people, claiming she was Black even though she had White parents and lived her childhood as a White person. I take seriously the "I know when I see it" approach to group membership. People are members of groups when the relevant people accept them as members of the group. This is what it means to have group membership decided by relationships.

We now have three different approaches to identity. There is Rachel's view: racial identity as a personal choice. The worldview you choose to adopt and the culture you decide to immerse yourself in determines your identity.

Many of Rachel's detractors see race as determined by birth. This is an essentialist version of racial identity. Maybe it's genetic, maybe it's ancestral heritage, but it's in you at birth. From this perspective, Rachel lived a version of *Get Out*: a White woman created a Black body to inhabit.

My view is that race exists in relationships. What people in a relationship accept as true determines identity, and the reason they accept any given truth is irrelevant. From this view, racial identity exists in and must be conferred by a community.

From my perspective, Rachel's identity is a function of her relationships. Rachel was born White, became Black, and then became a "not-Black" woman who wanted to be Black. She is Black if, and only if, she believes she is *and* she lives in a community of Black people who accept her as such. Assuming she honestly saw herself as Black, while Black people accepted her as Black, she *was* Black. The moment that other people who were defining her as Black rescinded her membership, she was no longer Black in that community. At the same time, I don't think she was White because she refused to accept this identity. She occupied a liminal space, a kind of racial purgatory suspended between unreconcilable relationships.

Whatever you believe about Rachel's identity, the strength of the negative response to her is telling. People care about the integrity of group boundaries. It really upsets people when they think others are pretending to be something they're not, especially when it threatens the integrity of a group they belong to because a threat to the integrity of the group is a threat to the social world the group's members built and inhabit, and a threat to the selves of people in the group.

FAMILIARITY WITH THE IDEA OF race makes it a useful example. But its ubiquity can also make it difficult to see what I mean by the social construction of groups. A different example might allow us to see the nature of social construction more clearly, and the value people place on social groups.

In 1957 a device was invented that had the potential to "cure" deafness. The device, a cochlear implant, would ultimately take about twenty more years to be released for general use, but the announcement of its existence radically altered the prospects for those with hearing impairment.[44]

This is a commonly used medical device nowadays, but the way it changed the lives of some of those who had them implanted is still moving to witness. There are videos of people hearing their name for the first time breaking down in tears. Children implanted with the device have less trouble learning to speak and do better in school. Not surprisingly, after it was proved safe for young children, many parents were eager to have this device implanted in their children.

Given these benefits, it might be surprising to hear that the National Association of the Deaf did not see this medical device as a miracle. In 1991, the organization wrote an official statement that derided the research and the device. The statement raised a number of concerns, but most relevant for us is this:

> There is now abundant scientific evidence that, as the deaf community has long contended, it comprises a linguistic and cultural minority. Many Americans, perhaps most, would agree that as a society we should not seek the scientific tools nor use them, if available, to change a child biologically so he or she will belong to the majority rather than the minority—even if we believe that this biological

engineering might reduce the burdens the child will bear as a member of a minority.[45]

Some deaf people view themselves as connected to other deaf people through the shared experience of the absence of hearing and the way they navigate the world as a result. The hearing impairment creates relationships that in turn give way to a sense of community, and this community provides social identity. Seen this way, it's not surprising that some in the deaf community do not embrace cochlear implants. When you understand the absence of hearing as the marker of membership in a community—rather than a biological deficit—the rejection of implants starts to look like the response to Rachel Dolezal by the Black community, an attempt to maintain the integrity of a valued group.

Perhaps even more so than race, we can agree that the deaf community is defined by an objective fact: in this case, the inability to hear. Yet some see this as a physical impairment to be fixed and others as an essential feature of the self. What you see in the statement above is a group defending its existence. What for some is a miracle cure is, for others, a potential elimination of an integral part of their self. This is what it means to be a part of a group: to know your self through communion with others, and to guard the boundaries of the community that define you.

IF YOU'VE EVER PEOPLE-WATCHED, YOU'VE probably felt that you can tell something about where people are from just by the way they walk or sit or eat or some other simple act of moving through the world. Of course, you can also use more obvious clues like what people prefer to eat, the way they dress, or if they are walking around like tourists, but I'm talking about something more subtle: the way people carry their bodies, certain subtle accents, the way they express emotion, the way they interact with objects and people around them.[46,47]

Social identities exert physical influence on the way we encounter and engage with the world. This is true for all of us. The way you and I sit, walk, and eat is unique to us, but it also bears the mark of groups to which we belong. Male friends in some Arab countries walk holding hands; if you're Ugandan you probably walk more slowly in a group than when alone, but if you're American the reverse is probably true.[48] We don't have to think about these things; it's just the way we behave. Groups shape and define us.

It's hard to overstate the importance of social groups. In places that emphasize the priority of the individual as the primary building block of human existence, social groups can feel like constraints to be avoided. Indeed that word, *constraint*, points to one important role of groups: groups help define selves.

Imagine what you would be without connection to social groups. Your mother would be the person who gave birth to you, but the idea of mother and child would not exist. These things, mothers and children, are social categories, not people. To be a mother is more than giving birth; to be a mother is to be connected to the bundle of rights and responsibilities your culture uses to define the category. Research that looked at the differences between motherhood in the US and in China finds that the way people parent differs between cultures. US moms scored higher on warmth/acceptance and encouraging democratic participation while Chinese moms scored higher on encouraging modesty and maternal involvement. Cultures shape the way the role of motherhood is expressed, and by implication what it means to be a mother. What it means to be a son or daughter, mother or father transcends any single relationship. These identities exist as social constructions.[49]

We value our inclusion in social groups and zealously guard their boundaries, protect them from perceived outsiders. In this way we resist efforts to weaken their meaning, to undermine the stories they tell, stories that connect us to others, the past and the future. We do this sometimes even when others devalue the identity or use it to harm us. Women, the deaf, Black people, the Jewish community, each of these groups faces threats from groups with more resources or power, yet many members of the group still deeply value their group membership.

Being part of the group gives them connection—a whole category of people from whom they can understand themselves. If I experience discrimination as a member of a group, I can place that experience within a worldview shared by people with the same experience. We can collectively define the meaning of our shared experiences. People can tell stories of the strength and perseverance of their community in the face of powerful evils. In fact, evidence suggests that greater psychological connection to a group can protect the self-esteem of individuals who belong to discriminated-against groups.[50]

The jump from thinking in terms of isolated individuals to individuals in relationships is a quantum leap. This shift allows for the birth of self. Social groups take this a step further. Social groups provide structure that makes it possible for us to live in a world that far exceeds our face-to-face interactions. Social groups go beyond raw, idiosyncratic relationships and allow us to spin myths to give our relationships deeper meaning, to extend and expand our lives, to shape our reality. Myths that gain power in our telling and retelling of stories of who we are and how we came to be. These myths organize the social world and help us locate selves, including our own, within it. The stories we tell allow us to transcend the absurdity and potential meaninglessness of life as a finite, isolated individual.

But as we will see, this comes at a cost.

# 7

## In or Out

When we present ourselves as men or women—via things like our dress, speech patterns, and gestures—we are asking that we be treated in accordance with an identity that a particular community agrees on. We all understand the parameters. But those rules and boundaries aren't a given; they were created and have evolved over years. To say that I am a man is to accept a concept of manhood that preexists my claim to it. To say I feel like a man or woman requires that these identities exist in sufficient detail that I can imagine what they feel like. What does it feel like to be a man or woman? Or think about it this way: How do you *know* what it feels like to be a man or woman? Maybe you infer the inner experience of an older sibling, family friend, or parent based on their behavior and the way others respond to it. Maybe you get it from watching TV or movies. You watch a show and see everyone swoon over a thin person in a red dress, and you see yourself, or at least hope to. I must be able to (or want to) see my self in others who occupy my preferred identity, in the way they walk and talk, laugh and cry, in the way they relate to others. You *learn* to feel like a man or a woman. Sure, you know what it feels like to be *you*, but that's not the same thing as what it feels like to inhabit a social identity.

When I walk out on the street, people typically assume I'm a man. My secondary sexual characteristics—facial hair, muscle development, hip shape—have something to do with their assumption, but so does the way I've been socialized to dress, speak, and behave. My way of being, and the way the world that I exist in is organized, makes it easy for others to accept my preferred gender identity without question. For me, it feels like people just see *me*. I have no experience of asking to be seen as a man. Not everyone knows this ease of being unquestioned.

ON FEBRUARY 12, 1968, AFTER a Memphis, Tennessee, city garbage truck crushed Echol Cole and Robert Walker to death, despite repeated concerns about the safety of the trucks the city used, Black sanitation workers in the city went on strike, carrying now-iconic signs that read "I Am a Man."

What were these signs about? Few people would doubt the sex of the people holding these placards; they clearly appear to be male. Taylor Rogers, a participant in the march, recalled, "All we wanted was some decent working conditions, and a decent salary. And be treated like men, not like boys." The placards in that way included a demand for change in social relationships, for the rights associated with manhood.[1]

In 2022, Lia Thomas, a swimmer for the University of Pennsylvania, won her first Division 1 national championship in the 500-yard freestyle. Yet rather than giving her a massive round of applause, the crowd, according to ESPN, was noticeably quiet as Lia took the podium with her trophy. Lia is a transgender woman, and with that win became the first transgender athlete to win a Division 1 national championship in any sport. Much controversy has surrounded Lia and other transgender women in sports, with many opponents claiming that their biology gives them an unfair advantage. The same year that Lia won her championship, the NCAA announced midseason that it was abolishing rules in place since 2011 that had allowed trans athletes to compete on teams or with competitors who match their gender. In the first few months of 2022, almost two dozen US states introduced bills that ban trans women and girls from competing in women's sports.

There is an inherent contradiction in these two examples: a trans woman's biology is enough to deny her the rights of womanhood, yet a group of males holding up signs saying "I Am a Man" reveals that access to manhood requires more than biology—for the strikers in Memphis it required fair treatment at work to feel a true part of the group. These two examples demonstrate that while you can assert your preferred identity, you cannot determine your social identity on your own. Whether your biology is thought to match your gender or not, as a social identity, gender hinges on others' acceptance. We don't let people be: we participate in their being.

The current debate about gender identity highlights the power of structure and the limits on our freedom to be. Whether we like it or not, whether it's fair or not, much of our social life is touched by gendered distinctions. The universal experience of sex and gender, and current challenges to the way we understand gender, make this domain an ideal space to explore the boundaries of social identity. Understanding just how fluid gender can be—and, at the same time, understanding just how much these fluid distinctions end up shaping individual lives in the real world—is a route to better understanding the malleability of all social identities. Genders and families, nations and ethnicities: all of these are only as real and important as humans decide they are.

My approach to this discussion requires us to clearly distinguish between sex and gender. I use *gender* to refer to a social identity, and *sex* to describe a feature of biology. The relationship between sex and gender has two components: necessity and sufficiency. On one hand, many people believe the "correct" sex is *necessary* for manhood and womanhood. This is why some people would deny transgender women access to women's sport. On the other hand, a person's biology is not *sufficient* to qualify a person for full membership in a gender group. This is why the sanitation workers could carry signs that read "I Am a Man" and have everyone understand what they meant. The difference between necessary and sufficient can create confusion around this topic.

Manhood and womanhood require more than biological sex. To be a "real" man is to be powerful and respected, to be *attractive* to and *attracted* to women, to be insensitive to pain, to be rational rather than emotional, to be able to provide for and protect your family. To be a "real" woman is to be maternal and concerned about others' well-being, to be *attractive* and *attracted* to men, to be sensitive and communicative. These ideas of manhood and womanhood aren't etched in stone; they depend on place and time. The ideas shared in a community create the meaning of manhood and womanhood.

To say this another way: people have ideas about masculinity and femininity, ideas that define manhood and womanhood that go far beyond a person's biology. Yes, biology might affect you if you are held to the expectations of masculinity or femininity, but biology alone does not guarantee the rights, or incur the expectations, tied to manhood or womanhood. To be a man or woman, or any other social identity for that matter, requires that people engage with you as a member of the group. This makes the broadly accepted definition of the group terribly important.

In 2020, in response to an article titled "Creating a More Equal Post-COVID-19 World for People Who Menstruate," author J. K. Rowling tweeted, "'People who menstruate.' I'm sure there used to be a word for those people. Someone help me out. Wumben? Wimpund? Woomud?" Her response sparked outrage in various corners; it was read as transphobic, excluding trans women from the category. After the initial backlash, Rowling explained her views via a blog post and multiple tweets. Here is a sample of what she wrote:

> If sex isn't real, there's no same-sex attraction. If sex isn't real, the lived reality of women globally is erased. I know and love trans people, but erasing the concept of sex removes the ability of many to meaningfully discuss their lives. It isn't hate to speak the truth. The idea that women like me, who've been empathetic to trans people for decades, feeling kinship because they're vulnerable in the same way as women—i.e., to male violence—"hate" trans people because they think sex is real and has lived consequences—is a nonsense. I respect every trans person's right to live any way that feels authentic and comfortable

to them. I'd march with you if you were discriminated against on the basis of being trans. At the same time, my life has been shaped by being female. I do not believe it's hateful to say so.[2]

I want to highlight that, for Rowling—at least at the time—the debate seemed intensely personal. She believed that the denial of sex was tantamount to denying *her* lived experience as a woman. Furthermore, she rejected the idea that the identity "woman" is a social creation. She writes on her blog that "'woman' is not a costume. 'Woman' is not an idea in a man's head," and takes issue with terms like "menstruators" and "people with vulvas" because to her these words feel "hostile and alienating."

Rowling's position at the time seemed to capture the thoughts of many. To be a woman is surely to be something more than an idea in a man's head, but what is this "more"? Some would be satisfied with a purely biological definition, but as Rowling demonstrates, some find this demeaning. I'd state her position as *womanhood is a lived experience tied to biology*. This position is reasonable in part because it's true that being born female often seems sufficient to experience life as a woman. The way we look is often the first thing that people use to determine our gender. If you appear to be female there is a good chance you think of your self as a woman and will be treated as such. The crux of the situation, though, is whether being born biologically female is *necessary* to live as a woman—my position is that it is not. I reject the idea that we locate womanhood in genitalia or find its essence in any other aspect of biology. Womanhood and manhood—gender—lives in our relationships, not in our bodies. To be a man requires that you think of your self as a man *and* be treated like a man by others.

Research on perceptions of gender support this anti-essentialist view. In one study people were asked to judge characteristics of people based on images of faces. Importantly, the faces were chosen such that some were categorized as women, some as men, and some gender-neutral. The gender-neutral faces were categorized half the time as men and the other half as women.[3] That we can't always tell if a person is a man or woman doesn't mean that we aren't looking for an essence, just that sometimes it might be hard to discern. However, in this study when people were shown the gender-neutral face after a masculine face, the gender-neutral face was more likely to be seen as a woman. When a gender-neutral face was shown after a feminine face, it was more likely to be seen as a man. It seems that people make relative judgments of gender.

Relative judgments of gender point away from the idea that we are responding to the gender essence of the people we encounter. You are seen as a man or a woman compared to others, *not* because people correctly identify your essence. Our judgments of people's gender are affected by the social setting in which we make them in combination with the attributes of the people we judge. Even if a gender essence exists—I don't believe it does—we are not perfect detectors of it.

What's necessary and sufficient to be a woman is that people engage you as a woman. And what it means to engage you as a woman differs across settings, but people know it when they see it. It might mean having a door held open for you; assuming you aren't good at math; treating you as physically fragile; assuming you're good with kids; expecting you to wear a dress, headscarf, or heels. The reasons people believe you to be a woman are irrelevant, but emerging research goes against the idea that our behavior is only driven by the biology of those we judge.

MANY OF US HAVE A sense of our "true" identity. We just know who and what we are—we feel it in our bones. Rachel Dolezal knows she is Black. Lia Thomas, the champion swimmer, knows she is a woman. But sometimes other people don't see us the way we see our selves. The possibility of a mismatch between people's sense of their identity and others' view of them points to what's at stake in defining social groups. It's nothing less than who we are and can be.

This is, in part, the genesis of the movement to state our preferred gendered pronouns. We provide pronouns to eliminate the need for assumptions regarding our preferred gender identity. When we state our pronouns, we seek to separate the socially expected appearance of gender from the conferral of identity. It attempts to create space—the feeling of freedom—by reducing the demands made of people to inhabit others' understanding of their preferred identity.

But there is something of a conundrum here. The statement of pronouns places considerable weight on a shared understanding of gender. When I state my pronouns, it allows me to separate my preferred gender identity from my appearance, and maybe your assumptions about the way gender should look, but it doesn't tell you what it means to me to be a man or woman. Stating pronouns doesn't challenge the importance of gender; it is a request for inclusion in the "correct" social category. This is a much different goal, for example, than trying to abolish the use of gendered pronouns or challenge the concept of gender altogether.

The intimacy of gender, its connection to our bodies and the breadth of its consequences, highlights the power of the social construction of self and the plasticity tied to it; if identities are constructed in relationships, shifting the way people relate to each other changes their identities.

CONSIDER THE WAYS COMMUNICATION TECHNOLOGY has affected the way we relate to each other. Imagine the shift in what was possible with the advent of the written word: the ability to transmit a thought or feeling without face-to-face interaction. Consider the shift when these records became easy to transport across long distances. The ability of hundreds of millions of people to read the same information, the ability to transmit a thought, faithfully, across thousands of miles and years. These shifts changed who we could be. It led to the idea of national languages—a common language codified in writing—where before there had been many regional dialects. This change in language produced a hierarchy of speech, which gave language groups greater social meaning and, hence, power. And all of this affected the political formation of today's countries.

In his influential book, *Imagined Communities: Reflections on the Origin and Spread of Nationalism*, Benedict Anderson argues that the printing press allowed for the foundation of nation-states. In this account the importance of the press was not the dissemination of information per se, but rather the experience that the information was shared. The belief that you are sharing my experience allows me to imagine you as part of the community I belong to. You and I are reading the same material in the same tongue, which must mean we are connected. These new imagined communities became nation-states. As Hugh Seton-Watson, another scholar of nations, defined it, "a nation exists when a significant number of people in a community consider themselves to form a nation, or behave as if they formed one."[4,5]

Whether you find this story of the birth of nationhood compelling is not important. What I want to focus on is the idea that nationhood requires the ability to *imagine* us as a meaningful community, and one argument is that the production of the nation as a meaningful community relied on a technological advance that allowed for large numbers of people to share information and to *know* it was shared. By affecting the ways we connect, technologies shape selves, social groups, and the way the world is organized.

Before the idea of a nation took hold there were large numbers of people living under common political entities, but these entities were not nation-states, and arguably not even coherent communities. In a few centuries we went from a world dominated by empires to one that consists almost entirely of nation-states. This transformation was nothing short of a global shift in consciousness. The idea of the nation-state has proved an irresistible force. Today nation-states shape the selves of billions of people.[6]

The idea of political self-determination through the creation of nation-states is among the greatest examples of an idea's ability to transform the world. The adoption of the idea of nation-states, an imagined community of selves, as a legitimate basis for demands of political rights shaped the modern political era. "The People"—the imagined community of the nation—has become a, if not *the*, legitimate basis of political power.

The idea of a shared sense of rights created such a profound connection among constituents that the psychology of community is written into the formal constitutions of nation-states. And it's not just the "We the People" of the United States. Here is the preamble to the current constitution of France:

> The French people solemnly proclaim their attachment to the Rights of Man and the principles of national sovereignty.

The Constitution of the Russian Federation:

> We, the multinational people of the Russian Federation, united by a common fate on our land, establishing human rights and freedoms, civic peace and accord, preserving the historically established state unity.

And here is a portion of the Constitution of the People's Republic of China:

> The People's Republic of China is a unitary multi-national State created jointly by the people of all its nationalities.

Each of these charters claims that power flows from "the people," rather than, say, a divinely appointed leader. The idea of "the people" in each case is bounded—"We the people of the United States," "The French people," "the multinational people of the Russian Federation," "the people of all its [China's] nationalities." Each also tacitly acknowledges the need for freedom and structure. In the first three examples, individuals' rights are mentioned explicitly. In the case of China, the emphasis is squarely on structure.

The idea that many millions of people scattered across immense expanses of land constitute a meaningful group would be incredible if it weren't so mundane. People who speak a variety of languages and dialects have come to feel connected because they or their ancestors were born within a boundary, sometimes a boundary created centuries *after* their ancestors settled the land.

In the same way that gender can seem an objective feature of the natural world, the idea of nation might seem primordial, because for much of human history collections of similar people formed meaningful entities, tribes, and clans. But like the concept and performance of gender, nation-states as we know them today are a social invention. Nature doesn't dictate the content or conferral of social identities.[7]

I reject the notion of biological essentialism as the basis for social identities. But the freedom from biology offered by the social creation of identity comes at a cost: we can't claim that we were born knowing or feeling our gender, that our parents' genes dictate our race or nationality. Social identities aren't truths written on our souls or in our genes. Who and what we feel ourselves to be must come from relationships. What that means is that your self is the result of the way people in your life relate to you.

When our perceptions of our selves and others' perceptions of us align, things are easy. People seem to spontaneously see the "truth" of who we are. But when a desired identity that is crucial to our sense of self is not validated by others, we come face-to-face with the reality that we cannot simply choose to be whatever social identity we want. Protestors insisting on their manhood, transgender women fighting to access women's bathrooms, immigrants fighting for recognition in their adopted nations are just a few examples of people fighting for the dignity, and sometimes safety, that comes from having others affirm their identity.[8]

IT'S NOT ALWAYS A BENEFIT to be conferred an identity. Social identities come with rights *and* responsibilities. Stereotypically, men are expected to mow lawns, take out garbage, and physically defend loved ones. Women are expected to cook, clean, and care for sick loved ones. Failure to uphold expectations tied to social identities, failure to live up to the often-unstated responsibilities tied to an identity: these are punishable offenses. The people and communities that confer these identities will withhold benefits or mete out punishment: women might not be provided physical protection, men might not be given the deference they might expect.

In a study I published with colleagues in 2022, we found that members of racial groups were more likely to consider and treat women of their own group like "real" women, as compared to women of other racial groups. How did we know? First of all, evidence is clear that women are punished for violating gender norms. For example, when women managers behave the way we expect a typical boss to behave (e.g., with directness and confidence), they are rated more negatively than when they behave more gently. In our study, we presented people with descriptions of women with names typically associated with White, Black, or Asian women, and described a situation in which the women behaved like a typical boss or like what people expect of women. We found that the typical tendency to evaluate agentic women more negatively than communal women was weaker when people evaluated women from racial groups other than their own. In other words, people don't seem to mind as much when women from other groups violate expectations of women.[9]

In another study we examined responses to Hillary Clinton's United States presidential candidacy. We measured anti-woman gender bias among Whites and ethnic minorities in the United States. Both groups reported roughly the same amount of bias, but the effect of the bias on the way people responded to Hillary Clinton differed by people's race. The more bias White people reported, the less likely they were to vote for her. Meanwhile, ethnic minorities' gender bias did not predict whether they would vote for Clinton.

It seems people have fewer problems with women outside their own racial group who violate gender expectations, by doing things like running for the US presidency. My collaborators and I believe this is because people outside their racial group don't see them as *real* women—biologically female, sure, but *women*, no. They don't, in other words, confer them the rights or responsibilities of womanhood. Therefore, they aren't punished for violating feminine standards. Consistent with this idea, in a separate study my colleagues and I found that people have an easier time identifying gender-related words after seeing photos of men or women of their own racial group. It seems that photos of women and men of other racial groups don't activate thoughts tied to gender as strongly as members of our own racial groups.

WE ARE CREATED IN COMMUNITIES, so when our communities change, so do we. New relationships can produce new communities that confer identities that define selves. Take a benign example: when a new music genre develops, early adopters create a community around their shared interest in the new music. Growing up in the 1980s and '90s, this was rap for me and many of my peers. I listened to rap music evolve over my formative years, from rappers like the Fat Boys and Kid 'n Play, to Eric B. and Rakim, BDP, Public Enemy, and Run-DMC, through N.W.A, Tupac, Wu-Tang, and Biggie, alongside a host of other artists. Like most communities the culture was greater than any single component. The music was important, but there was also graffiti, dance, and fashion that gave shape and expression to the culture. To be a member of the community required more than liking the music. As it evolved, it would solidify what it meant to be a "real" member of the community, what the new identity entailed. To be a member required that you knew and adhered to the norms and expectations of the community, that you adopted the symbols and markers of membership. This was in the language used, the way to walk, not just having the "right" clothes, but wearing them the correct way. Also, existing communities decided their relationship to this new identity group and "helped" define its borders. At the time the call to label the music "vulgar" helped cement its rebel status. Many young urban professionals (yuppies) decided that hip-hop was to be ignored or denigrated as unintelligent and violent.[10]

The community you belong to, or the one you'd like to belong to, provides access to a social identity in a certain context that you may not have access to in another. You can be someone in one place and someone else someplace else. For example, my local hip-hop community might accept me as a legitimate member, but that wouldn't guarantee that a hip-hop community in New York would accept me as such. This conditionality is true of all identities. You can be a man who wants to be a woman in one setting, say a place that rejects trans-identities, and be a woman in another.

Think back to Rachel Dolezal. I claimed that Rachel was White, became Black, and then became a not-Black person who wanted to be Black. She sought out affirmation for her sense of self as Black by creating relationships within the Black community. Rachel went to what many would consider extreme lengths to constrain her self in service of acceptance by the Black community. When this community accepted her as Black she became Black in that community. When this acceptance was withdrawn she ceased to be Black.

Identities conferred upon people by communities are not cost-free. Social identities are constraints. Not only do social identities demand that you adhere to your community's standards, but the standards of the community also become standards for your self. I don't know anything about surfing, but if I identified my self as a surfer, and I became accepted as such, then evaluations of my surfing-self would become evaluations of my self. You can contrast this self-evaluation with someone who surfs, but is not a surfer: they do not subject themselves to the standards of surfers—indeed, they are free not to—but they are also not part of the community of surfers as a result.

To challenge the social identities within a community is to challenge the relationships that constitute that community. Let's stick with the surfing example. To claim to be a surfer in a way that challenges an existing identity challenges the self-understanding of the existing members of the community. If being a surfer comes to mean using a short rather than a long board, if it means only big-wave riding, people who don't fit this definition but identify as surfers will be upset. To treat these individuals as "nonsurfers" challenges the relationships that hold them together, the relationships that define them as surfers, that constitute their community.

It should be no surprise that communities protect the integrity of their social identities. And it should be easy to see how multiple communities develop. Maybe there is a big-wave surfer community, a short-board community, and a longboard community. I'm no surfer, but I do know that in the rap of my youth there was a (sometimes deadly) rivalry between communities defined by East Coast and West Coast rap.

Communities define the meaning of identities. To be Black or a woman is to be so in a particular community. When we say we are this or that identity, we are referring to our understanding of what it is to be that identity as it exists in some community. This can take different forms: our identities are defined and created in our workplaces, volunteer organizations, schools, and even sports teams. When I think of myself as a man, it's not a man the way it would have been understood in ancient Egypt or Greece, or even present-day communities, such as religions or nations that are unfamiliar to me. I am a man, or not, as understood in and accepted by my family and friends, people at work, and in other pockets of community.

Over time and between communities, social identities are fluid. They can transform and evolve. In some Western cultures what it has meant to be an ideal woman has shifted between curvy, waif-like, and athletically toned. What it means to be a beautiful woman—what it means to be a woman at all—shifts, excluding some women at one time and place and others in different places and times.[11]

The fluidity of boundaries means that communities can reject or accept requests for inclusion in the identities they create. What happens when new claims are accepted? Claims like Dolezal's, like the protestors holding signs saying, "I Am a Man," like the trans woman competing in women's collegiate sport? The request for inclusion is not an individual request; it's a request to change the boundaries of group membership, and therefore the meaning of the identity. If people accept Rachel as a Black woman, it changes what people believe is necessary to be Black. If Rachel can be Black, then having White parents is no longer a barrier to membership in the Black community.

I know who I am as a Black person because I understand the boundaries of Blackness. When these boundaries shift it challenges my understanding of my self. If Rachel is Black, maybe it weakens relationships I have or might form based on the perception of shared heritage. The Memphis sanitation workers' demand to be treated as men, and Lia Thomas's participation in women's sport: these are challenges to group boundaries, and therefore challenge relationships rooted in the racial hierarchy and gender roles, respectively.

People care deeply about the integrity of their group's boundaries. When social identities do not function as you believe they did or should, the structure that made sense of the world, that made sense of *you*, starts to fray. If gender organizes many of your relationships, which it does for lots of people, a shift in your understanding of gender is a profound challenge to your sense of self. When it seems to you that men are no longer men, and women no longer women, it's easy to experience a bit of vertigo. Not only is my sense of self as a man or woman challenged, but the way I should engage men and women shifts, because what it means to be a man or woman is embedded in the way we interact within and across gender categories.

When J. K. Rowling wrote, "If sex isn't real, the lived reality of women globally is erased," she is highlighting the implications of boundary change: to shift the boundary of womanhood, to challenge the importance of sex in the definition of woman is to threaten the reality of all women. To include trans women would disrupt her identity, and that of the women she believes share her experience. She also explicitly states that her position is not anti-trans; it's a defense of the boundaries of the existing category. From this perspective, exclusion is not the point, there is no animus here, exclusion is a by-product of maintaining the integrity of the group.

The same sentiment might explain some Black folks' anger toward Rachel Dolezal. Her claim to Blackness challenges shared realities that they believe define Black identity; maybe it's shared childhood experiences or the absence of choice about being Black. If Rachel's claim to group membership violates shared realities that people believe define their relationships to the group, her claim challenges their understanding of themselves. When we believe a person's claim to an identity violates tenets that bind the group, it would be a surprise if it wasn't taken personally and forcefully challenged. Every claim to a social identity becomes a communal claim.

Your social identities depend not only on the acceptance of the communities to which you claim membership, but also on the experiences that tie you to the group. Those shared experiences create the relationships that define the group in the first place. When you encounter someone claiming group membership who doesn't share an experience critical to your understanding of the group, it not only challenges your understanding of the group, it challenges your ties to the group and your understanding of *your* self.

That's why even if you're fine with the breakdown of the traditional sense of gender—even if you think it's a long-overdue deconstruction of a suffocating social system—you should be able to see how disorienting a change in that understanding can be for others. Even if you think immigration reform and better treatment of immigrants is long overdue, you can see how it challenges others' sense of self. When it seems any foreigner can come into the country and be counted a citizen, it can challenge people's understanding of the national community. Changing the makeup of the people accepted into the national community can disrupt some people's sense of place in the community and change their understanding of their selves as members of the nation.

Challenges to the boundaries that define social identities are not only challenges to people's ideas, beliefs, or principles— they are challenges to people's *selves*. If we exist as islands unto ourselves, beings fully contained within our skins, why care so deeply, so personally about the identity of others? The personal is political because the self is social.

WHAT SHOULD BE CLEAR NOW is that lone individuals can't define social identities as they see fit. Communities give social identities their power. But these communities can also create pain because individual freedom is, by definition, constrained by *social* identity. Being left out of—or, maybe worse, being cast out by—a community is an incredibly painful experience. But the need for structure, to exist in relation to other people, requires limits. Without inclusion *and* exclusion there is no social structure. To be a woman or man, White, Asian American, or Black, German, or Swiss or any other social identity requires acceptance of a shared view of these identities, not a freely chosen construction of self.[12]

There are some identities we just seem to feel in our souls. For many people, gender falls into this category. But how could you have known what it was you felt the first time you felt it? Without other people, you couldn't know what that feeling meant. Without other people, you would just *be*, but whatever you were, it wouldn't include a social identity. Our ideas about who we are flow from relationships that existed before we did; they reflect connections that ground us in the past.

We enter a story already underway. We are who we are because of what came before us. To feel your gender or any other social identity is to be connected to something that preceded you. The ideas of manhood and womanhood, race, nationality, class, and many other social identities are pregnant with meaning created over generations. These identities were created and live in relationships, and structure the world we live in. To feel any of these identities is to participate in a history you have only a partial awareness of.[13,14]

The experience of manhood and womanhood we have today was built and refined by our ancestors. Just a few generations ago, in 1969, trans activist Virginia Prince popularized the term *transgender*, giving people who felt born in the wrong gender a word to define themselves and a group of people with whom to relate. What it means to be transgender has evolved since then to be more inclusive. At the time, Prince used the term to describe people who felt the wrong gender, but who did not opt for gender-confirming surgeries. "I, at least, know the difference between sex and gender, and have simply elected to change the latter and not the former," she wrote. Now *transgender* is considered an umbrella term that encompasses people who do and don't opt for surgery as well as some nonbinary and agender people. Prince and other transgender pioneers created and refined, through social interactions and relationships, social identity boundaries that transgender people today use to understand their community.[15]

Our selves, the structure that helps us make sense of the world, limit what is possible. The social is always constraining. You can only be what is made available to you by relationships. The range of possibilities might be vast, but you cannot occupy any of them alone.

# 8

## (Re)Writing Self

In March 2021, Jimmy Fallon had TikTok influencer Addison Rae on *The Tonight Show*. At the time, Addison had approximately 81 million followers on TikTok, who largely tuned in for her rendition of whatever viral dance was popular on the app. The premise for her visit to Fallon's show was an attempt to teach him eight of the most popular dances, to hilarious effect.

Soon after the episode aired, the bit sparked significant backlash. It's important to note that Addison is a young White woman, and that many of the dances she highlighted on the show that night were created by Black dancers and choreographers. Critics pointed out that Addison was given the opportunity to go on TV to represent the work of minority artists, without crediting the original creators. As part of this conversation, many noted that this fit easily into a long history in America of White people benefiting from the work and creations of ethnic minorities. The episode had clear echoes of using images of White people as cover art for Black musicians' albums. Just as it's easy to understand that record companies believed they would sell more music to their White customers if album covers featured White people rather than the actual Black artists, it's easy to see how Addison, rather than the actual creators, ended up on the show. The show wanted to maximize its audience and Addison was quite popular.

Addison's popularity points to an unfortunate reality of the current version of the internet: the way it is set up reinforces existing social prejudices through things like a focus on photos and videos, and selective exposure based on past behavior and algorithmic predictions. The dominance of visual information on the internet and on the apps we all use allows people to express their preexisting biases for and against visible social groups, whether they know it or not. On social media today you are bombarded with photos and videos, some serious, many deeply silly, most benign. Often what people are presenting is an image of who they would like to be. This creates a situation in which the audience can relate, or not, based on who they are or would like to be. It's nice to see an idealized image of who you could be.

Think of your social media feeds. I'd bet they're curated to reflect people who look and think like you do. It's also nice to have your view of the world reflected to you by others, which often means the views of your social group. The average White person is more likely to be influenced when they watch someone like Addison doing a dance than when they see the actual creator, if that creator happens to be a person of color. In siloing ourselves online, we reinforce preexisting biases.

In a reality different from our own, the internet would open us to a range of ideas and people we normally wouldn't have access to. Instead, people are presented with information that confirms their existing biases, in part because algorithms (correctly) predict what people want to see. People prefer to be shown what they like, or sometimes what they like to hate. Unfortunately, often what people like does little to make the world a better place.[1,2,3]

The bias toward what we know, abetted by algorithms that use these biases to curate the options we can choose from, reduces the likelihood of growth or education. People thus remain in their tribes, thwarting and perhaps even pushing against the original promise of self-expansion and freedom that the early internet pioneers intended. In its current form, the internet seems better designed to give us the comfort of tribal connection over the freedom of possibility.

Neither the internet nor social media created the tendency in people to seek out like others or to prefer evidence that confirms their preexisting beliefs—there is considerable evidence that these biases existed long before the internet and social media—but these technologies supercharged people's ability to indulge these tendencies. Here again predictive algorithms serve to help us find what we want, and often what we want is to see an image of the world that fits our existing worldview.

So far, I've focused on the way relationships create selves, the way collections of selves—communities—shape the selves in them, and the way selves curtail our freedom. But what I'm really getting at here is this: Our need to make sense of the world and to have a recognizable place in it demands a self.

Today, what perhaps most structures and limits our world are two interrelated phenomena: technology and nation-states. Technology can be seen in the TikTok and television discussions above, while nation-states can be seen in how TikTok and television, Jimmy Fallon and Addison Rae, are distributed,

broadcast, experienced, and controlled. Both create and maintain social groups (such as gender and race) and both support
the other (below we'll discuss how technological innovation
spurred the creation of nation-states, and how nation-states
have cultivated tech).

But most importantly, both technology and nation-states
shape the way we experience our lives. Who controls who we
come into contact with? Who controls what we see? Who decides
which groups are valued, and which are denigrated? Nation-
states and technology together reveal how little control we have
over our own lives. To some extent we are all participants in a
study where we are merely allowed the *feeling* of freedom.

Scholars have claimed that social media and other technology enable echo chambers, in which people only hear what others like them want to say.[4] When faced with an overwhelming
number of choices it makes sense to choose what people like
you choose. When you don't know what to believe, it makes
sense to believe what people like you believe. In this way, it's
possible that more information makes us more reliant on close
relationships or trusted groups to make sense of it all, or at least,
to not have to try to make sense of it on our own.

The communities we are born into shape the environments
that sustain and shape us. The beliefs and behavior of the people
in your neighborhood tell you how the world works. You learn
about how to engage others by watching the way people around
you speak to each other, learning through interactions what it
means to demonstrate respect and what kind of people deserve
respect.

The influence of others on our selves flows up from more
intimate relationships to social groups, and it also cascades

down—social groups affect the selves we are and can become. To understand selves and freedom, it helps to examine the context that shapes groups. And technology is a major feature of that context.

FOR MOST OF HUMAN HISTORY, our interactions were face-to-face. Your life is likely a far cry from that now; you are connected to millions of people whom you don't know, and never will. You share and create realities with people thousands of miles away. Changes in communication technologies have fundamentally altered the human experience. It expanded our social contacts and flooded our world with information. Shifts in communication technologies, from clay tablets, to papyrus and paper, to radio and TV, to websites and streaming affect the way we interact with each other. Technology, in other words, has changed what and who we can know, what we are exposed to, and what we share.[5,6]

When people first began to connect to the internet, there was considerable excitement and optimism about the possibilities. This new medium was going to set us free. The anonymity would allow us to explore new selves. You could find supportive communities that might not exist in your hometown. Members of stigmatized groups could have voice; they could find community without having to reveal their personal identity. You could safely try out identities that friends and family might not support.

Early internet advocate Anthony Rutkowski, then a lawyer and engineer, said in 1996, "These technologies are going to profoundly affect the way we perceive our humanity."[7] Everyone has stories to tell and ideas to share, he said, and now they could. Beyond sharing information, though, people could share specific parts of their identities while keeping others under wraps. In a 1995 journal article titled "This Bridge Called My Mac: Lesbian Feminist Politics on the Internet," Emily Lloyd describes herself as having a "tragically feminine face"—tragic because she greatly desired to be perceived as a butch lesbian. On the internet, interacting with people who couldn't see her face, she could act out her butchness. "I can adopt a 'butch' screen name, sign on and be Butch for a Day," she wrote.[8]

People were also awed by the amount of information available to anyone with a computer and internet access. You could go online and find an answer to just about any question. You could learn to tie knots, play the ukulele, or just about anything else you could imagine. The internet could instantly provide news about places you'd never been. The only limit to what we could learn or know would be our imagination.

It's hard for me to remember, but there was a time when the internet promised unlimited personal growth. You can still learn just about anything, but people had originally expected more. People thought it would demolish barriers to understanding and create room for connections that were previously unimaginable. In retrospect, we imagined a revolution in human nature. I think it's safe to say that's not what we got. What we got instead was a stream of constant reminders of who we are: content curated based on our biases, tighter ties to people like us, and an inability to turn off or turn away from it all. The overwhelming amount of information available to us affects our ability to balance the need for a coherent stable self, and the feeling of freedom and possibility.

. . .

ONE OF THE MOST PROFOUND effects of technology is its ability to shape what we remember. The greatest thing and the worst thing about memory is its imperfection. We don't file away our experiences like books on a shelf or files on a computer, perfectly based on some complex Dewey decimal system. Our state of mind, our past experiences, the social context when we experience events affects the way we remember them. Think of the last time you felt famished. How was the food you ate in that situation? I'd bet it tasted great. How about the music you heard on a fantastic date? There is a reason couples have a song. The creation and retrieval of memories is not simply a recording and replaying of sensations, pictures, sounds, or tastes; the process is affected by emotions and motivations present at their creation and recall. Perhaps the most famous example comes from Proust's *In Search of Lost Time*, in which a sip of tea mixed with madeleine crumbs immediately and vividly brought to mind the old village where he grew up with his aunt, who would give him the same treat.[9,10]

An important feature of our current environment is the bargain-basement cost of digital memory. I like books and vinyl records. I don't have as many as some, but probably quite a bit more than most. Despite what I said earlier about the ease of transporting paper, anyone who loves books knows that moving a collection is a pain. Vinyl albums are even worse! Compared to the cost of digital books, music, or photos, the cost of acquisition, holding, and transportation of information in physical media is ridiculous. The cost of collecting and maintaining music and photos in physical form was enough to significantly limit the amount of data most people could, or were willing to, amass. Now, once we've purchased a mobile phone, we pay almost nothing for taking and storing pictures and music. So we keep untold gigabytes of it.

As I am sure you've experienced, sometimes when you pull up a memory you get it wrong, a fact that I become more aware of with every passing year. Turns out it's completely normal to misremember things. In fact, it's not that uncommon to have the feeling of clearly remembering something that never happened. Studies have shown how easy it is to produce these false memories through innocent-seeming suggestions.[11] Don't you remember that time you were playing in the clothes rack at the department store, and your mother walked away? You went looking for her, but you couldn't find her and started to cry. Remember that nice older woman who asked what was wrong and took you to a desk for them to call your mother on the intercom? Remember that? Turns out lots of people can, even though it never happened to them.

The fallibility of our memories has significant downsides—think about the cost of a mistaken eyewitness testimony—but at least one potential benefit is flexibility. The fallibility of our memories can ease the ability of the self to evolve. Many of us might want to forget early adolescent years. The way we looked, the way we acted, the awkward interactions that defined us: most of us do not carry this as the truth of our selves today. This goal-directed forgetting is happening all the time. What if the current glut of recorded information is impairing this process?

Pruning our memories, forgetting events and feelings, these things help us evolve beyond what we have been to become something new. The flux necessary for the feeling of freedom requires a break from the past. Our current technology provides a near-continuous stream of digitally captured memories, reflections of past selves, that follow us everywhere. These constant reminders of who we were might reduce the range of who we can be.[12]

Just the other day my phone curated a flashback of a trip I took a few years ago. It was great, all moving photos and soaring music. I loved it, but do we really want some programmer we don't know deciding—via algorithm—what we remember and how we remember it? Sure, it was nice to be reminded of those great memories, but what if they weren't that great for me at that moment—what if I'd recently broken up with, or lost, a partner or family member who was on the trip? I think that technological advances are generally good (I'm certainly no Luddite) and that they're hard to suppress even if you don't like them, but it's worth thinking very carefully about how—or whether—to integrate new technologies into the social fabric of our lives. If we are not careful, algorithms, and the companies that write them, will be in the business of curating our pasts for us. And the presentation of your past might limit what is possible in your present.

THE VAST AMOUNT OF INFORMATION online also creates a problem of choice. Despite what we might think, we don't do well with unlimited possibilities. Want to get news? There are the cable shows, late-night hosts, newspapers, podcasts, online outlets— all of which are happy to tell you what's happening in the world. Or their version of it. Want to watch a TV program or movie? There are countless possibilities on a large and growing number of streaming platforms. Want to date someone new? There are plenty of fish on dating apps. We are constantly faced with a deluge of options, and research has shown that we don't always do better with more choices rather than fewer. Psychologists call this "choice overload." The basic idea is that with too many choices, it's hard to make any decision at all. We have limited cognitive capacity and selecting the best option requires weighing too many possibilities. We are overtaxed, feel frozen, and therefore are unable or unwilling to choose.[13]

Corporations are happy to help us with this problem. Major platforms track us, analyze our data, and predict our preferences using algorithms that rely on our past behavior and those like us. The outcome? They can then limit the options presented to us to those we *should* like, meaning those options they are selling that we are most likely to interact with.

It's easy to appreciate the simplicity provided by predictions offered to us, especially when they're pretty good. The problem is that we will encounter fewer truly novel choices. We are fed options that match who we have been. Maybe it's always been tough to step out of our comfort zones, but today it's possible that we spend less time grappling with the existence of scary side streets that might lead us somewhere new and exciting. Our freedom to choose, if such a thing exists, means less if the options we see have already been curated for us.

When the internet was new, people had little direct information about people on the other side of the screen, other than what their partners self-reported. This physical anonymity was key to some of the early optimism about the new medium. People who were usually disregarded could have their opinions heard absent identifying details that previously excluded them from the conversation. Perhaps the vaunted ideal of free speech would finally be tied to some degree of equality of platform, we thought. This could have led to the democratization of the

internet. This could have led to recognition of the value created by oft-stigmatized groups. But as we saw with the Jimmy
Fallon incident, it didn't.

Large social groups and those with significant political
clout who have dominated traditional media, not surprisingly,
continue to dominate newer forms of media. When new platforms come out, they prioritize lucrative popular consumption,
leaving smaller groups behind. This is how Addison Rae, the
White woman featured on *The Tonight Show*, becomes the face
of choreography created by people of color. This has a number
of unfortunate but predictable consequences, one of which is
that many people miss out on expanding their social network.

THE WAY WE TALK ABOUT technology today can give the impression that relatively recent innovations, like the World Wide
Web in 1989 and the first iPhone in 2007, represent cataclys-
mic shifts, which might be true, but they certainly weren't the
first. So, let's examine an older technology less burdened with
the weight of current controversy.

Think about paper. As we discussed, the invention of a plen-
tiful and easily portable writing surface (papyrus, parchment,
wood pulp paper) revolutionized the human experience. In a
book published in 1943, Dard Hunter, a historian of papermaking, suggested that human development can be divided into
three major stages: speaking, drawing, and printing.[14] The last,
printing, allowed people to record their thoughts with a fidelity
that memory can't come close to matching and to disseminate
those ideas on a scale that was previously unimaginable.

Paper allows you to "speak" to people you might never
see, people long dead, or those not yet born. Paper allows for

continuity of thought, which allows for collective efforts on a large scale. People can build on others' ideas. The ability of the Roman Empire to operate such a vast bureaucratic entity was greatly aided by control of the papyrus trade. After conquering Egypt in 30 BCE, taking control of the papyrus trade led to an explosion of writing. This also allowed for the dissemination of political pronouncements, contracts, and cultural practices across the empire.

You can trace the explosion in scientific ideas from the eighth to the fourteenth century in the Islamic world to the adoption—or wartime appropriation, depending on the story—of the Chinese method of paper production. During this time scholars from all over the Old World translated existing knowledge into Arabic and wrote manuscripts that allowed for the integration and dissemination of this knowledge. Among a number of other intellectual and artistic advances, Arabic numerals were widely adopted, algebra was invented, and Aristotelian thought was recovered and reintroduced to the Western world. Paper changed what people were capable of by expanding the way they could connect.[15]

Changes in the way we engage and connect have profound consequences for who we are and can be. First there was paper, which let us write down ideas. Then there was the printing press, which allowed us to distribute them at scale. Now, thanks to the internet, we can send ideas out into the world almost immediately. Your thoughts are just a tweet away from an audience. At each stage technology shifted how we could connect and how many people we could connect with. Paper allowed us to extend in space and time beyond our physical limits, the printing press created communities on a scale that was previously unthinkable, and the internet has allowed information to traverse vast distances instantly and given many the potential to reach an audience of billions.

To this point, we have focused on the way people make sense of and create each other—the development of self in families, the importance of groups, and the creation and conferral of identities like race and gender. We now see that technologies like paper and the printing press are crucial in allowing those selves to expand across space and time. Advances in communication technology allowed for interaction with more people, which expands the pool of possibility our selves emerge from by giving us access to almost infinite potential relationships. In addition to close personal relationships and small-scale communities, we are also subject to vast social systems that may not entail ever interacting with other people face-to-face.

The first weekly newspaper was printed in Germany in 1609. By the 1620s, newspapers were a regular feature of the daily life of many literate people.[16] This allowed people to read, at least those who could read, the same information as hundreds of others each day. For the first time, huge swaths of people were connected to a single version of unfolding history. The ability to imagine others sharing the same information and political circumstance, an ability made possible by the printing press, moved us from parochial local identities to identities tied to massive social groups over expansive territories. These communities became governable entities, nation-states, defined by bonds among selves that constituted a national identity and eventually a sovereign state.

The founding of a nation-state is an exercise in storytelling. These stories create and explain boundaries. They cast a net over a collection of people and proclaim it a community; songs are written to tell of their glorious birth, monuments are erected to the men who founded or defended their nation, magnificent buildings are constructed in styles that connect them to their mythical histories. They become the children of immense empires, luminous city-states, or powerful kingdoms. Rome becomes Italy, Ionian city-states become Greece, Pharaonic dynasties become Egypt. Yet, as we've noted earlier, nation-states as we know them today were only born in the last two hundred years or so.

Despite their recent invention, nation-states dominate the global political landscape. You may or may not feel tightly connected to the nation of which you're a citizen, but you almost certainly recognize that you've been shaped by it. The boundaries of nation-states are often understood as lines that define cultural differences like language or religion. These boundaries then organize economic activity, educational systems, justice systems, and an array of other institutions. These institutions structure our lives.

It might sound strange to suggest that nations exert more influence on the self than, say, life partners or family. Your immediate family is typically the first direct influence on your existence and long-term partners might be the most consistently present, while the "nation" can feel far away. Many of us only engage with the nation when we read the news or vote, but today nations provide the context in which social groups like political parties, families, and professional and educational identities exist.

Nation-states exert incredible influence over the context that shapes the operation of more intimate relationships and communities. They set the rules for the way we exchange goods and labor, the support new parents can expect to receive, the way we educate our kids, how much time we are allowed to spend away from work, and countless other aspects of our lives that affect our relationships. Nation-states provide the background against which relationships are created and play out.

To fully understand the influence of the nation-state, we should start with how the State defines inclusion in the community, which can often be ambiguous. For example: Who counts as a woman? Who counts as Black? In contrast, nation-states can formally define membership in the State. In the United States, there are five ways to attain citizenship: you can be born within the boundaries of the State; you can be born to US citizens; you can marry a citizen; you can serve in the military; or you can be naturalized. Other nation-states use different criteria, and nations can and do change their criteria. For example, if you were born in Ireland before January 1, 2005, you are an Irish citizen by birth. If you were born in Ireland after that date, your citizenship depends on the history of your parents or grandparents.

Citizenship entails connection to the national community through the institutions and products of the State, such as public schools, transportation infrastructure, health insurance, national parks, the postal system, and federal banks. Just as with other social identities, this identity contains rights and responsibilities. For example, citizens must pay taxes to support the State. In return citizens are eligible for access to social goods produced by the State.

Membership in national communities allows the nation-state to exert considerable power over people's lives. This power is often explicit. If you don't pay your taxes, you're likely to hear from a government agency about significant financial penalties and possibly jail time. If you break a legal contract, you run the risk of being sued in the State's legal system and losing a significant sum of money. If you are accused of criminal activity, as defined by the State, you might find yourself on the wrong side of officials with guns. The ability to uphold social rules with force is a particularly powerful tool of the State. The State can take away the ability to perform certain jobs by declining to issue you a license, it can take away your physical liberty by putting you in jail, and it can take your life through the operation of officials on the street (police) or through more drawn-out legal processes (the death penalty).

The State's ability to use force is so core to its existence that social theorist Max Weber defined the State as a community that claims a monopoly on the legitimate use of physical force.[17] But the power of the national community—a group of people who feel connected to each other, rather than just people governed by the same rules—goes far beyond direct interaction between the institutions of State and citizens. The true power of the State lies in its ability to shape individuals' beliefs, by which I mean the national community's beliefs about the way people should interact.

In 1986, the United States Supreme Court upheld the constitutionality of a Georgia state sodomy law that made oral and anal sex between consenting same-sex adults illegal. In a dissent, Justice Harry Blackmun wrote that the Court did not just "refuse to recognize a fundamental right to engage in homosexual sodomy; what the Court really has refused to recognize is the fundamental interest all individuals have in controlling the nature of their intimate associations with others."[18] In this and a slew of other rulings, the United States demonstrated its interest in defining and shaping the national community's understanding of acceptable interpersonal interactions. What kind of relationships do "we the people" deem legitimate? The State legitimizes certain behavior and relationships, which allows them to be seen as normal, while casting those outside these designations as punishable. Even more importantly, it treats certain actions as inappropriate to even consider among "true" citizens, thereby shaping the wider community's cultural values.

Control of legal institutions allows the State to affect what people—the nation—perceive constitutes appropriate intimate behavior, and this extends to what constitutes a legitimate family. There is no reason a household must be defined in terms of a heterosexual "nuclear family"—mother, father, and children. Sure, having kids requires the biological contribution of sperm and ovum, but the ability of a couple to conceive doesn't dictate the structure of households. Yet some nation-states have formalized marriage as a union between a man and a woman exclusively.

I find the success of the fight to legalize same-sex marriage interesting for a host of reasons, but I want to highlight two. First, the goal was to extend the definition of marriage to include a legal connection between two people of the same sex, not to push the State out of the business of validating familial relationships. People recognize the power of the State and wanted access to the social benefits that such legal acceptance of their relationships provided.

Second, the desire for inclusion in the rights the State affords married couples put pressure on the existing connections in the excluded communities. If your community is defined by rejection of the dominant narrative, if membership in the queer community entails the belief that marriage is a way to perpetuate the patriarchy or an attempt to stifle romantic freedom or choice, to accept marriage as defined by the nation-state can be read as assimilation that weakens the boundaries of the group. In other words, maybe the acceptance of gay marriage shifted the boundaries of the gay community.

The cost of mainstream acceptance might be a change in the way your community defines the self. If queer communities are defined by the shared rejection of the existing standard model of romantic relationships, what becomes of the community and your self once you're accepted by the mainstream? Is the gay and lesbian community the same if mainstream acceptance of gay marriage represents a loss of its "outsider" status?

STATES MUST ENFORCE RULES, BUT the strongest, most effective states avoid the use of force whenever possible. If the people don't voluntarily embrace the State's rules, the State has lost control of the nation. Imagine if people only followed the rules of the road if they thought they would get caught; the road would be chaos. It's just too costly to effectively watch people all the time, so states depend on people voluntarily following rules.[19]

A state can control a nation through extreme surveillance and force, but it's very difficult to control the way people in a community interact with each other through force alone. The use of force is likely to disrupt the smooth operation of relationships and all the benefits that flow from such interactions. Consider all the social goods that are created in the complex, smooth, (mostly) voluntary interactions among people. You can drive a car without fear of someone smashing into you at any moment, you can drop your kids off at a building and expect them to be well cared for by professional educators, and you can pull out a card or cash to pay for goods or services and expect people you've never seen before to accept your payment without question.

The creation of a business is a study in the way the State can ease interactions between people. For example, the legal framework that allows enforceable contracts lowers the cost of distrust. People know that they can count on the State to recoup costs if a partner doesn't uphold their end of an agreement. This allows people to more easily work together to create valuable goods and services, which increases the quality of life in a community. States function most effectively when they bend the experience of reality—what people can conceive of—to shape the way people interact without the use of force.[20]

In their most powerful form, nations elicit a willingness to sacrifice. It's the connections to others, the idea of who you are with these others, that these others constitute part of you, that allows people to suffer and even die in the name of the nation. When you identify with the nation, to die in service of the nation is to die to live on; if the nation persists, despite your physical death, so does your self.

Nations can be particularly powerful, but they operate just like other big social groups. When you think about a nation you likely think of a physical place, but a nation does not require land. If tomorrow your country was overrun by invaders, and they claimed the land as their own, would your sense of connection to your nation cease to exist? I'm pretty sure it wouldn't.

Your nation might no longer exist on international maps, but the nation could and probably would continue to exist as an idea among national patriots. You would be a part of a stateless nation.

History is full of examples of national movements seeking to become self-governed nation-states. In 2017, politicians in the Catalonia region of Spain declared Catalonia an independent nation-state. The Spanish government subsequently declared the referendum unconstitutional. For significant parts of human history, Jewish people have defined themselves as a nation without a state. Today a number of peoples identify as stateless nations, including, but certainly not limited to, the Romani, the Québécois, the Navajo, Kurds, Tamils, and Tibetans. A nation is the community of selves tied to each other by the *idea* of nation. All the rest (e.g., flags, shared language, anthems, even geography) merely serve to bring or hold the selves together.

Defining a nation in terms of "the people," a singular concept, raises the question of divisions among the people. In a state based on the will of the people, how do you create and maintain solidarity of a diverse people? The easiest thing to do is give preference to the most powerful group, but this weakens the State if it creates committed dissidents. A number of nation-states have been harmed by a political minority group's ire. The Tamil Tigers in Sri Lanka, the Irish Republican Army (IRA) in the United Kingdom, and the African National Congress (ANC) in South Africa are just a few political movements that openly challenged the nation-states their community lived in.

Political discussion within states is often riven by the question of who should be counted among the elect, who should benefit from and control the State. A nation-state must find a way to define its people broadly enough to be politically viable and powerful, but also maintain clear enough boundaries between who is and is not one of "the people" to remain manageable.[21]

Many nation-states are at least partially defined by a racial or ethnic majority, in that some group exerts greater control over the apparatus of the State. This group controls a disproportionate share of State offices, benefits more from the educational opportunities, experiences less use of police force, fares better in the criminal justice system, and on and on. The nation-state is often structured by this group to maintain the group's dominance. In some cases this can be accomplished by relying on a decision-making rule that favors the dominant group. For example, voting might be limited to the dominant group. In the United States voting was originally limited to a relatively small set of White, property-owning men. In other cases, the dominant group might rely on maintaining control of valued resources and what people think constitutes legitimate access to these resources. It might also focus on establishing decision-making rules that allow a minority to block the will of the majority through mechanisms like requiring a supermajority, say two-thirds, of the available votes to make legislative changes. In all of these cases, the move to maintain the dominance of "the people" demonstrates the importance of social selves, often defined in racial or ethnic terms, within the operation of the nation-state.

Acceptance into the group that controls the institutions of the nation-state affects whether you will enjoy the rights and freedoms pledged to the people. Will you be protected from random violence? Can you expect a full share of benefits apportioned to citizens? If the nation-state you are a part of has a racial-ethnic component, and you aren't of the dominant race or ethnicity, you might have citizenship, but there's a good chance that you will not receive the same share of benefits of national membership as those with the "right" heritage.[22,23]

Across nation-states, research finds that members of the dominant racial or ethnic group in any given country have better education outcomes, make more money, and live longer than members of other groups. For example, in the United States, on average, White men can expect to live approximately four years longer than Black men. In another example, in Australia from 2018 to 2019 the Indigenous population's median income per week was roughly 65 percent lower than that of other Australians. This hierarchical structure appears to be baked into the nature of nation-states.

Just as a structure provided by a divinely ordained monarchy depends on the stability of a royal line of descent, the structure provided by a nation-state depends on a stable understanding of the nation. Questions about who counts as "the people" of a nation can precipitate crises—war, rebellion, or revolution. You can't have the definition of the nation changing with the wind. The definition of the nation is unlikely to undergo existential changes, changes in who counts as "the people," without a crisis. A shift in the selves that constitute the group, a feeling among existing patriots that their selves do not define *their* country, might be enough for them to destroy the country to save *their* nation.[24,25,26]

As I write this, and despite the continued dominance of White folks in the United States along most dimensions of economic and physical well-being, some White nationalists espouse White Replacement Theory. This is the idea that some shadowy elite have a plan to replace White Americans with ethnic minorities. This is an explicit concern about what kind of self defines the idea of American. In May 2021, Merrick Garland, the attorney general of the United States, testified to Congress that the greatest domestic threat facing the United States was "racially or ethnically motivated violent extremists"— "specifically those that advocate for the superiority of the White race." The power to define a community is not something people give up lightly.[27,28]

That some White Americans are willing to engage in violence to protect their belief that they are "the real" Americans reflects how strongly people tie their sense of self to national identity. You might ask why people care if there are more Americans who identify as ethnicities other than White. If people define America as White, the shift in demographics can be experienced as destruction of the nation. To have "those people" around is one thing; to allow them to overrun "our" country is something else. It's the same reasoning as J. K. Rowling's rejection of terms like "people who menstruate." Allowing the definition of men and women to shift disrupts the accepted understanding of gender and means having to rethink relationships defined by shared understandings of gender. The protection of the nation, the protection of gender, the protection of racial group boundaries is the protection of self.

IF YOU WANT TO SEE the effect of the State in people's lives look no further than where people live. In the 1940s, '50s, and into the '60s the Federal Housing Administration made it nearly impossible for Black families to buy suburban homes by restricting

Black families' access to federally backed mortgages. In contrast, White families left urban areas and moved to suburbs in droves, their new home purchases subsidized by the federal government. The result was large suburban communities of White people and urban areas stripped of resources filled with Black people. Decisions about where to place transportation corridors also affected the viability of new communities, in some cases making it even easier for people who lived in suburbs to commute to work in cities, in other cases running through urban communities creating noise, pollution, and destroying communal spaces. The implications of these two influences alone continue to reverberate through individuals' lives from cradle to grave.[29,30]

Where one lives is the primary source of that person's interactions and relationships, the self-defining mechanisms we have come to understand throughout this book. Who would you have been if you were born somewhere else, surrounded by different people, in an environment rich with resources or one stripped of what you grew up enjoying? I mainly grew up on the south side of Chicago. I had the good fortune of going to some schools that had the resources to provide me significant educational opportunities. In high school when I began skipping lots of classes, an administrator showed great interest in me, which helped me stay on track. In college a faculty member suggested I consider getting a PhD in psychology. In graduate school my advisor taught me to see the world through the lens of psychology. Each of these people shaped the course of my life. Would the life I live be possible without these influences that cascaded from the good fortune of my early circumstances?

Almost certainly not. I am the sum of my circumstances, and the people who came into my life as a result of simply where I *was* at any time.

THE FEELING THAT WE ARE what we are and would have been regardless of circumstances helps the winners to claim more credit for success than deserved and allows those on the losing side to believe that they can change their fortunes through sheer force of will.[31,32] The reality that much of what and who we are is a product of where we are and who we are around complicates these claims of deservingness. The idea that our outcomes are solely a result of talent and effort is absurd on its face. If people really believed this, there would be much less anxiety about, and money spent on, trying to give kids every conceivable advantage in the race for status. This is not to say that people don't differ in talent or effort, or that these differences don't affect outcomes. But to say that these are the only two determinants of people's outcomes is ridiculous, and to say that they are the primary determinants is only a little less silly. If the same person could be born in Vietnam and in the United States, certainly their outcomes would differ. I would go further and say that if two different people were born in the United States, and the same two different people were born in Vietnam, the differences between the two sets of people would not be the same. In other words, it's not only that people's opportunities differ across nation-states, but within nations people are not ordered along the dimensions of intelligence and work ethic. Reliable differences between groups that differ only in their *social* construction give these claims weight.

The idea that differences between groups created by the

State are somehow not generated by the operation of the State is nonsensical. To explain group differences without reference to the operation of social systems, especially those tied to the State, would require a belief in an essentialist nature of groups—some are innately better, smarter, harder working. Either the group differences reflect the operation of social forces or the groups differ in some biological way that accounts for the difference. If groups are social constructions, as I've been arguing, the inequities—both the disadvantages and advantages— can't reflect groups' innate characteristics, because social groups don't have innate characteristics.

WHILE IT'S UNDERSTANDABLE THAT PEOPLE would not want to have personal choices dictated by the State, they often misunderstand the true power of the nation. To be defined by the nation is to accept certain limitations that accompany membership in any social group. The patriots who decry State overreach fail to recognize that their patriotism signals an abdication of freedom. To behave as if national identity can exist without a cost to freedom is to misunderstand the nature of both self and nation. Whether or not the State allows you to buy guns or tries to force you to get a vaccination is a reasonable concern, but the real power of the State lies in its ability to require that you hold certain beliefs in order to define your self as a patriot. In some quarters to be a true American patriot is to believe in the United States' fundamental goodness, to believe that it is exceptional in all domains. These beliefs require a degree of willful blindness that is incompatible with a recognition of alternative possibilities necessary for freedom. To blindly follow, to blindly support speaks against freedom. But perhaps this freedom is a price people are willing to pay when they see their group, and hence their selves, as among the elect.

Stay with me here. I think it's important to make one more point about the intersection of power, identity, and perspective. Some groups have the power to treat their view of the world as objective or neutral. This view from Nowhere often just happens to serve, or at least appears to serve, their own group's interests. Meanwhile, other groups' positions are presumed to emanate from their social identities and are, therefore, less "rational" or neutral. We can make a distinction between "from" and "for": all political positions emanate *from* some identity, but not all positions necessarily are *for* the interests of the petitioners' social groups.

The use of the phrase "identity politics" to capture the interests of some groups demonstrates the joint operation of power and identity. If we understand politics as decisions people make, individually or collectively, about the governance of relationships between people and groups of people, then all politics are identity politics. Decisions people make are rooted in who they are because who they are shapes their perception of the world. There is no such thing as a social view from Nowhere.

As I've been arguing throughout this book, we are all—every one of us—located in social space. We all have social identities, and these identities affect our preferences. We all make judgments from somewhere. That's not to say that we can't think carefully about our positions, or that all positions are equally valid, but when someone disparages another's view as coming from a particular social perspective, we should be immediately skeptical. The idea that people are influenced by their identities is, by itself, a faulty foundation for criticism because it applies to everyone, including, especially so, the critic.

When our judgments dictate the way people should be governed, where we stand carries considerable weight. In the realm of politics, we make decisions about the allocation of collectively created social goods and the costs associated with their creation. We decide on the way we collect resources (taxes) for the common good, how to prioritize competing social needs, the nature and range of the freedoms people should enjoy, and the limits on freedom that people should endure for the sake of security. The decisions we make affect the way people live and die. Given the importance of these decisions, I don't think it's too much to ask that people consider where, exactly, they stand when they make them.

# PART III

# You

## *and*

# Everything

# 9

## What's It All For?

If you ask people what makes life meaningful, they might list things like family, friends, health, or their occupation. It's certainly the case that these things can provide meaning, but I want to go a little deeper. Why do these things provide meaning? What do we need for life to feel meaningful? You probably will not be surprised to hear that I think meaning is something we create, and that at the crux of meaning is the self and the feeling of freedom.

When I think about the meaning of my life, the first thing that comes to mind is death. Where we end can help us see more clearly where we've been, and what took us to our destination. Do we leave with regret? Do we leave with a resigned sadness or satisfaction? Maybe we're just happy it's over. The way a journey ends can clarify the journey itself.

I wish for myself a graceful death, at home, in relatively little pain, surrounded by loved ones. In some cases, people take a more active role in the way their life ends. People go to war knowing that they might die in the line of duty. And, in the most explicit example, people take their own lives. Most people avoid an active embrace of death, but making a choice to die can tell us something about the experience of the meaning we imbue life with.

On June 11, 1963, at a busy intersection in Saigon, Buddhist monk Thích Quảng Đức set himself on fire to protest the persecution of Buddhists by the South Vietnamese government. The day of his death, Thích got out of a car and sat on a cushion placed in the road for him as a fellow protestor poured flammable liquid over his head. He then recited a prayer and dropped a match on himself. Eyewitnesses said that onlookers wailed, and that some, including police officers there to control the demonstrating monks, prostrated themselves in front of Thích's burning body. The moment was captured in a now-iconic photograph— Thích sits serenely in the middle of the road, engulfed in flames as a large group of fellow monks and citizens watch.

The following week, four more Buddhist monks and a nun followed his example and committed suicide in the same public way. Thích Quảng Đức's act is considered an important precipitating event in the eventual fall of the Diem government. The photo of his burning body was seen around the world, and the international reaction it created put considerable pressure on the Diem government, which eventually acquiesced to the Buddhists' demands.

On December 17, 2010, Tarek el-Tayeb Mohamed Bouazizi, a twenty-six-year-old vegetable vendor in Tunisia, poured paint thinner on his body and set himself aflame in front of the local government office. Authorities had allegedly harassed Bouazizi for years; on the most recent occasion they had taken his vegetable cart and scales and slapped and insulted him. Just before dousing himself and striking a match, he reportedly yelled, "How do you expect me to make a living?" His act was by most lights one of frustration. Still, within hours, his self-inflicted death led to protests that eventually culminated in the ouster of the man, Zine al-Abidine Ben Ali, who had ruled Tunisia for twenty-three years. Bouazizi remained in a coma after the incident and died less than a month later, but he is remembered for being the start of what came to be known as the "Arab Spring," a series of political movements against authoritarian regimes throughout the region.

What, then, does it mean for someone to choose to end their life? What can it reveal about the nature of meaning and life? Though the monk and the vegetable vendor both committed the same physical act, there is an important distinction to be made. As Thích Quảng Đức burned he sat lotus style, calmly, as the flames consumed his body. He appeared to be shockingly impervious to the external world, even while his body was literally on fire. The monk planned and coordinated a spectacle around his death meant to extract as much effect as possible from the act of taking his own life. Of course, others then responded to this act by making meaning of his life; after his death, he was revered. Today there is a statue in Ho Chi Minh City to recognize his sacrifice.

In contrast to Thích Quảng Đức, Tarek el-Tayeb Mohamed Bouazizi's act was that of a person who seemed to place little value on his life, or maybe more accurately, who felt that others had drained the meaning from his life to the point of finding it not worth living. The vegetable vendor's story sounds like that of a person who feels trapped by social forces outside his control. A life constrained by external circumstances to the point of desperation. Maybe what he lacked was the feeling of freedom. Perhaps the visibility of the constraints he faced—the inability to sell his produce, to provide for his family, to protect himself—robbed him of the will to live. In some ways, maybe setting himself aflame was an assertion of freedom.

The monk's life might be what many of us have in mind when we think about a meaningful life, one in which a person feels in control of their own destiny and chooses to dedicate their life to something more than their own comfort or physical pleasures. Perhaps you imagine monks serving a noble cause or taking joy in the completion of simple tasks. It's not the life for all of us, but it's not hard to imagine others seeing meaning in a monastic life. You might see the monk's life as admirable and the vegetable vendor's as regrettable, but despite these differences, they both inspired major political changes. Both of their lives *came to mean something.*

These two things—the meaning *made of your life* and the meaningful *experience of living it*—are very different. The meaning made of your life can be constructed retrospectively, after the fact, from discrete events that made up your life. The ability to do this is not the same as experiencing life as meaningful as you live it. To make meaning of your life after you're dead is a task others take on, maybe on your behalf, maybe for themselves, but it doesn't provide you meaning during your physical time here. In other words, your self can come to have meaning after your physical death even if your time on earth might have felt meaningless. But here let's focus on this question: Does life, as you're living it, feel meaningful?

• • •

FOR ANYTHING TO BE MEANINGFUL the world must make sense. The world must be orderly, and we must be able to locate ourselves in it. This limits the freedom available to us, and the amount of freedom we are even likely to tolerate. As we've discussed, complete freedom is probably unattainable. Complete freedom, if understood as the state of being unaffected by social influences, might be incompatible with our humanity. To be human is to be able to relate to other people as a human being; immunity to social influence precludes this ability. Others don't merely show us who we are, they define who we are, and the tensions among our multiple selves can tear at our, for lack of a better word, souls. People can tear our souls apart. As Sartre wrote, "Hell is other people!"[1]

The very same relationships and interactions that make you *you* also make it clear that you cannot be completely free in the presence of others. A feeling of being trapped might make you want to run from unnecessary relationships, or entanglements that tie you down. But there is little reason to expect avoiding others will lead to a meaningful life. Without others or the constraints they provide, life would lack coherence; *you* would lack coherence. And there is no meaning without coherence.

If you could choose freely, would you even want to? How would you even know what to choose? Consider my choice to become a college professor and all the choices I had to make to accomplish that goal. To say that I chose freely would be to ignore all the influences that friends and family had on me and my sense of the social costs and benefits of the choice. We hope to make *good* choices, choices that lead us to the outcomes we hope for. We want our choices to be tethered to the world in all sorts of ways. Research suggests that meaning in life is associated with the experience of purpose. To have purpose, our choices have to be tied to something more than our moment-to-moment existence.

When I talk to people about the importance of meaning in life, they sometimes respond that to care about such things is a privilege only of those with money, those who have their survival guaranteed without much thought or effort. But I reject this idea. Yes, there are people who worry about how to pay the bills or just find enough to eat, but why assume that they don't also care about the way they live or what their life is about? The idea that people only care about meaning after "lower level" needs are fulfilled assumes that meaning is a luxury as opposed to something that almost all humans strive for. I'd argue we all care about more than just the present moment. You don't have to consciously think about or voice the question of meaning in life for it to be present. Your life feels meaningful or it doesn't whether you bother to look closely or not.

And there is good reason to look: people who report that their life feels meaningful are seen as more appealing by others, show lower rates of psychological disorders, experience slower cognitive decline, and live longer. Given the importance of the sense of meaning in life, we might ask what it is. Here is one definition offered by psychologists:

> Meaning is the web of connections, understandings, and interpretations that help us comprehend our experience and formulate plans directing our energies to the achievement of our desired future. Meaning provides us with the sense that our lives matter, that they make sense, and

that they are more than the sum of our seconds, days, and years.[2]

Here is another:

Lives may be experienced as meaningful when they are felt to have a significance beyond the trivial or momentary, to have purpose, or to have coherence that transcends chaos.[3]

These definitions capture important themes in the psychological understanding of meaning, and two should jump out at you. First, meaning is associated with connections. The second theme is time. Both definitions explicitly note the importance of something beyond the present moment, something more than the mere sum of our time on earth.

These two themes, connections and time, tie meaning to the ideas of self and freedom. Connections provide coherence. You know who and what you are in the context of social connections. The connections that create self also tie us to people in ways that can transcend place and time. For instance, to be a citizen of a nation is to move beyond the trivial or momentary. You become part of the nation's history and help construct its future; it's a part of you and you are a part of it. There is a promise of a kind of immortality in the connections that create self.[4]

We must be able to discern structure in the world around us for meaning to emerge, and we need to be able to relate to this structure in some way. This requires a point of view, and a point of view requires self. We construct selves to give coherence to a chaotic world, in order to create meaning. Selves tell a story about the ways we relate to others. When we need to make sense of the world we tell a story about our selves.

In his book *The Man Who Mistook His Wife for a Hat and other Clinical Tales,* Oliver Sacks recounts the experience he had with a patient suffering from serious memory impairment. In a state sometimes referred to as Korsakov's psychosis, Sack's patient, in order to deal with his inability to make sense of things around him, continually constructed a world based on who and what happened to be at hand. One day when Sacks entered his room, the patient offered him cuts of meat, thinking the doctor was a customer at his deli. Sacks then let Mr. Thompson know he was not a customer, at which point Mr. Thompson pivoted instantly to believing the doctor was an old friend from the horse track. After realizing that wasn't quite right, either, he noted the doctor's white coat and believed him to be a butcher. And this goes on, worlds are spun out of bits and pieces of information projected onto the doctor. This patient was creating a social self from moment to moment, always in relation to the doctor or at least who he needed the doctor to be. Sacks observes about Mr. Thompson, "He must seek meaning, *make* meaning, in a desperate way, continually inventing, throwing bridges of meaning over abysses of meaninglessness, the chaos that yawns continually beneath him."[5]

What Sacks's example demonstrates so well is that we are not simply predisposed to see patterns; we are motivated to see structure. Without structure the world would be nonsensical, an "abyss of meaninglessness" beneath our feet. Meaning gives our actions content. It makes what we do *about* something. It elevates us above actions necessary for the bare minimum of survival. Even if all we can do is survive, structure is necessary to answer the question, "What are we surviving for?"

We enter life not at a beginning, but midstream. The currents and eddies that swirl around us—the stories about our physical place, groups we belong to, rights we enjoy, and responsibilities we must shoulder—don't fully determine who and what we are, but they do nudge us as we make our way. These stories shape the relationships that define us. They provide group identities that locate us in social space. They give power to states that control collective, and hence individual, action. They give us scripts for our most intimate relationships. The cultural forces that act on us play an important role in the constraints that give life the feeling of coherence. To this we add our own idiosyncratic relational experiences, our family dynamic, our friends and rivals, and our romantic partners. All together a coherent world emerges.

While coherence is necessary, it's not sufficient for the experience of meaning in life. We all go about our day acting on the world in all sorts of ways. We do laundry, we cook, clean, we work and play. Most of these activities are utterly forgettable. We don't think of them as important or as adding meaning to our lives. They are mere maintenance. We like to feel like we are going somewhere, but many activities in life feel like running in place, or maybe circles. Life can be coherent *and* aimless.

Life feels more meaningful when we have goals, things we want to achieve. If I get up and run today, and tomorrow, and the day after that, in the future I'll be more fit. The desire to be more fit in the future gives my actions today purpose. Think of it as asking the question, "Why am I doing this?" If the answer is because it needs to be done, the behavior is less likely to contribute to the experience of meaning in life than if you have a future-focused goal.

At this point you might be asking an important question: "Why does any goal really matter?" The feeling that the choices we make, that the things we do matter is probably the most important thing when we think about the experience of meaning in life. The real question when we think about meaning is, "Do our lives amount to anything?"

The idea that we matter means that our actions transcend the simple acts we engage in. We don't just act on each other; we affect ideas like justice, dignity, human possibility. Our actions transcend their immediate aims. My life is worth living in a cosmic sense. I am a part of something universal and my life contributes to this whole. This question of whether our life is meaningful might just boil down to whether we believe we are connected to something bigger, the sense that we have an important role to play, in some grand drama, or whether we believe that what we are experiencing right this second is all there is. Martin Luther King Jr. said, "If you've got nothing worth dying for you've got nothing worth living for." The belief that the arc of history bends toward justice requires faith, a belief in something unknowable, that there is a larger structure that we play a bit part in.

I was reminded recently about the importance of creating structure as an act of meaning making in and of itself. A man at a dinner party told me a story about living in San Francisco during the AIDS epidemic. He was living in the Castro, which was, and still is, a popular neighborhood for gay men. The 1990s in San Francisco was a grim time in the Castro; AIDS, then considered the "gay cancer," had started spreading throughout the community in the early 1980s, and by the '90s it had taken a heavy toll. The once-popular gay bathhouses were shut down and San Francisco's Gay Freedom Day Parade became more subdued. The disease was evident in the gaunt faces and thinning hair of many residents.

The man I talked to described running errands in the neighborhood and discovering the loss of his neighbors: the barista at his favorite coffee shop, the florist, the neighbor he ran into every Saturday at the grocery store. AIDS seemed to be touching every corner of his life. Many of his closest friends were diagnosed with HIV and were subsequently maxing out their credit cards for decadent trips and partying as if there was no tomorrow.

Eventually the storyteller himself was diagnosed with HIV. The first thing that came to mind when he found out he was sick, he said, were his tomatoes. Every spring he planted potted tomatoes and carefully tended them with great anticipation. When he was diagnosed, he wondered whether he should even bother planting the tomatoes that year. If he planted them, he would need to spend considerable time caring for them, even though he believed there would be little chance he would be able to enjoy eating them.

Although his circumstances were extreme, his situation has features that are quite common. Think about how often you sacrifice the current moment in the hopes of something in the future. Muhammad Ali once famously said, "I hated every minute of training, but I said, 'Don't quit. Suffer now and live the rest of your life as a champion.'"

Training for a boxing match, tending tomatoes, studying for a course, going the extra mile at work: all these things can be understood as sacrificing a bit of life now for the promise of something—the life of a champion, a doctorate degree, a big promotion—in the future. Understood this way, the value of the act depends on an outcome. It would be a waste of time, and precious life, to care for tomato plants if you knew no one would enjoy their fruit. This is one way to understand a component of meaning in life. The value of life *depends on goals achieved.*

But despite the odds, my companion did live long enough to benefit from effective treatments for HIV, and to tell me his story. By his account the answer of what to do with his tomato plants was obvious . . . of course he planted the tomatoes. It had nothing to do with optimism or trying to have something to live for. He said that after some thought he realized that eating tomatoes, though a delicious benefit, was never the point. The point of planting the tomatoes, the purpose, was the tending. He claimed to find purpose not in what the act produced, but in performing the act itself. Faced with an imminent end, he denied the importance of the future in giving an act purpose. The mere fact he was free to spend his time tending his plants gave the time he thought he had left a richness that would have otherwise been lost.

The idea that the freedom to *do* imbues acts, and by extension our lives, with meaning has a deep intellectual history. There is bracing optimism in the Viktor Frankl quote that "everything can be taken from a man but one thing: the last of the human freedoms—to choose one's attitude in any given set of circumstances, to choose one's own way." This quote suggests that we can choose our attitude toward life, and that this choice gives our lives meaning.[6]

Perhaps the feeling of freedom is important because we

associate freedom with ownership of our lives and purpose. If you can freely choose your actions or your attitude, your life is your own, and we want to feel like we own our lives. It would feel terrible to understand that others are controlling us, our actions and attitudes, by puppet strings. Even those who believe in an omnipotent God typically allow for the idea of human freedom.

The idea of freedom provides the feeling that at least some parts of our lives are our own. But maybe freedom of this sort isn't required for the feeling of ownership. Maybe all we need to take ownership of our actions or attitudes is the *feeling* of freedom. Maybe whether we can freely choose is irrelevant.

There is a classic psychological study from 1959 that illustrates the importance of the *feeling* of freedom, whether it's real or not. The study begins by asking a person to perform a terribly boring task: putting spools into an empty drawer, taking them out, and repeating. Each participant did this task for thirty minutes. Then they sat in front of another panel and turned each of forty-eight knobs a quarter turn clockwise, and then started at the beginning and turned them another quarter turn. They repeated this task for thirty minutes.

After the hour, the experimenter ended the study and asked participants if they could introduce the study to the next participant. This is the important part: the experimenter offers to pay the person either $1 or $20 to introduce the study by reading a script that says, "It was very enjoyable, I had a lot of fun, I enjoyed myself, it was intriguing, it was exciting." Nearly everyone agrees to introduce the study to the next participant regardless of payment. And, most importantly, the participants have the feeling of choosing. After the participant introduces the task to the next person (who actually works for the experimenter), they are interviewed about their experience. They are asked how enjoyable the task was and how willing they would be to participate in similar experiments in the future.

Here is the punch line: people who were paid $1 reported liking the task more and expressed more interest in similar experiments in the future than those who were paid $20. This study is typically used to describe something called insufficient justification. People paid $20 can explain their behavior because of the amount they were paid, but it's harder to justify lying to someone for $1. People will exhibit more commitment to a disliked task if they can't point to a reason why they did it. If I chose to describe a boring task as exciting, and there is no external reason for doing it, I must have actually thought it was exciting.[7,8]

What strikes me as interesting about the insufficient justification effect is that it shows that people can be led to see themselves as free, when from the outside it seems they didn't have any freedom at all. Maybe freedom is a matter of perspective—from the perspective of the person in the study they were free to leave the study rather than to lie to others about it. If we didn't know there was an experimenter pulling the strings, we would probably agree that they were free. The feeling of freedom does not require the absence of external influence, just an inability to see those influences clearly. And the feeling of freedom might be all we need for the experience of purpose.

Assuming the feeling of freedom is enough for purpose still leaves a problem. If all choices can have purpose and therefore contribute to meaning, how are we to decide what to do? The question of meaning is often asked to help us make decisions.

Will I have a better life—a "more meaningful" life—as an engineer or a cartoonist, if I have kids or not, if I move to another town or if I stay put? But if all actions have the same meaning, why plant tomatoes rather than take a lavish trip?

Consider two ideas that connect meaning to consequence in profoundly different ways. The first, called "weight," is that what we do today will reverberate into the future. In the most extreme version of this idea, everything that happens is destined to happen again and again in exactly the same way. In this universe everything you do has weight because you must be willing to do it again and again, forever. We can set aside this extreme version of eternal recurrence and allow weight to simply exist in behaviors that continue to reverberate through your relationships.

The second idea is that everything happens only once, and then fades away, eventually leaving no trace. Let's call this theory "light": nothing you do has any lasting consequence; everything passes against the background of an infinite, indifferent universe.[9,10]

The idea of "light" provides immense freedom. You live once and can do it however you want. All consequences eventually fade, and even if they didn't the indifference of the universe makes them meaningless. If the idea of being trapped under the weight of decisions and responsibilities is unbearable, you might like the idea of lightness. But if nothing you do has lasting consequence, is everything drained of meaning?

Carrying weight, on the other hand, requires a clear sense of self because the cost of most decisions lives on in your relationships. This is obvious in one sense: Many of our biggest decisions affect others. The decision to get married, the decision to have a child, to move away from friends and family—all of these decisions affect you and people close to you. To make decisions, you must first weigh your choices. If there are no future consequences of your choices, or if you don't think the consequences matter, what difference does it make what you choose? Choices that don't matter in the future are weightless.

MAYBE SIMPLY CHOOSING TO TEND tomatoes gives the act purpose and helps with the sense of meaning. But if you want to feel that what you do matters, that life is worth living in a cosmic sense, you need more than purposeful actions. The idea of an action mattering, of having *significance*, depends on the belief that it reverberates beyond the present.[11]

We might be able to break the relationship between time and purpose, as my gardener friend suggested. You've probably seen a sci-fi movie about living forever—they're easy to come across. These movies use a number of devices. In *Tuck Everlasting*, the Tuck family stumbles upon a magical spring of water that stops their aging forevermore. In *The Age of Adaline*, a freak accident involving a strike of lightning keeps Adaline twenty-nine eternally. However a story of immortality is pulled off, it always seems terrible to me. And usually, the moral of these stories is that living forever isn't as great as it seems. Would you really want to live forever? Where does that desire come from?

We want to believe that our actions have weight, that they extend beyond the moment of choice, that they continue to affect others. We want to believe that our selves continue to matter into the future. In a sense, then, the desire to matter is the desire to be immortal. We want some aspect of our selves to persist indefinitely. For some this might mean an attempt to preserve their conscious experience forever, through uploading their consciousness to the cloud or freezing their brain to be reanimated when medical science has the means to do so, as well as to cure what killed them and aging. But maybe what we really want is for our *selves*, rather than our physical bodies, to live forever. This might mean leaving a legacy via children or grandchildren, or perhaps some physical representation of their contributions, like a book or, if we have means, our name on a building. It can also mean connecting our self tightly to something that will persist after our physical death, like a philanthropic organization or our nation. If we are a part of something larger, something that we can imagine continues indefinitely, we can imagine our selves continuing indefinitely. This act of imagination gives us weight. We can imagine that our selves continue in the relationships people have with what we have created.

I am engaging with you as you read this and can do so whether I am physically alive or not. I regularly commune with authors who no longer walk the earth. The idea that we live on through social connections requires that we think beyond individual bodies to a social understanding of self. The more people report a sense of self-continuity across time, the more they say their life feels meaningful. And the more we believe that people close to us share our view of our selves in the future, the more self-continuity we report. In other words, *we can see our selves in the future to the extent that others see the same self.* Our sense of self is deeply affected by the perception that it's shared with others. We believe we are the self that we share with others.[12]

Social connections allow us to connect our present to the future; they help us create a sense of self continuity. If self exists in relationships, the sense of continuity should be related to shared expectations about the future. It is the sharing that gives the future a sense of reality and weight. When the monk lit himself on fire, he had a clear sense of the meaning of the act for a time past his physical demise. The hope for a better political future for his people, a hope he shared with his compatriots, as some of them followed his example in service of the same dream. He and the others engaged in the act of self-sacrifice with the hope of affecting others they cared about after they were physically gone. They projected their actions, and their selves, into the future of others. In an explicit statement of this self-into-other alchemy, Martin Luther King Jr. famously said the night before his assassination, "I've been to the mountaintop. . . . I've seen the Promised Land. I may not get there with you. But I want you to know tonight, that we, as a people, will get to the Promised Land." Notice he said, "*I* may not get there with you" but also said "*we*, as a people, will get to the Promised Land" (emphasis added). The "we" he refers to includes his self. By tying his self to the people he extends his self beyond his physical presence.

When the future has weight, the decisions we make have meaning, and so do our lives.

A weightless future can be a frightful thing, an ocean of unknowns that stretches out in front of us. We could imagine this is the future the vegetable vendor saw before him. We could live a life completely devoid of meaning, and at some point, our physical self will cease to exist: We will die. This existential threat to self can also pose a threat to meaning. Death is a physical break in temporal continuity. What can the choices we make now mean if it all will end, if everyone we know will eventually die? We all live in and contend with the shadow of nothingness.

As we've explored, people aren't content to just have a self, nor are they satisfied with just the feeling of freedom. In fact, the desire for meaning can be understood as a desire for more than just a physical self and more than freedom. To create a sense of meaning, the need for self must be *balanced* against the desire for freedom. Perhaps the feeling of meaning, then, is just a signal we've got the balance right.

# 10

# The End?

*Man is largely a social construct, and to deny a
man the social meaning of his death is to kill him
twice, first in the flesh and then in the spirit.*

—Gérard Prunier

The human body is a wondrous and terrifying thing. Bodies
provoke; they are beautiful and absurd. They sing and
dance, they sleep and dream, drink and eat. They get sick, they
break down, they grow old. To be human is to be an amazing, imperfect, flesh-and-blood body. We are animals, and our
physical existence can be glorious, but our bodies are also constant reminders of our frailty, our imperfection, our physical
impermanence.

The painful reality of the human condition is its inevitable
end, for all of us and those we are close to. This is the truth of
physical death: it is an end, one we can see coming but which
almost always feels far away or almost impossible to grasp. All

we've ever known, after all, is life. As you've aged, no doubt you've seen the signs. If you're lucky, as you moved from the body of a child into that of a teenager and adult, your body grew in strength and vigor. But at some point your body begins to decline. You lose flexibility, strength wanes, skin slackens. What was once easy becomes increasingly difficult.

When you say someone died, everyone understands that you mean the person's *body* has expired. What's not said, but implicitly claimed, is that the person *is* their body, or at least that their self can't exist without a living body. As we've learned here, though, the self is not the body. In terms of life and death maybe the self is *like* the body. Meaning, maybe the self doesn't die all at once. Parts of your self flicker briefly and then pass while other parts of your self last a lifetime. Some deaths of self pass painlessly or even joyously; other deaths can feel like they are tearing you apart.

My partner recently retired and at her party I remarked that a retirement feels like the combination of a funeral and a baby shower. One aspect of the self is dying, but something new, someone new, is being born. Your self as lawyer, doctor, or teacher is ending, but your self as gardener or French-learner is coming into existence. Old relationships will fade and new ones will be born. It's the same for graduations, moving out of your parents' home, getting married, and having kids. It's also true that a divorce, the physical loss of a life partner, or death of a parent is the end of one self and the beginning of another. Why should the balance between life and death, the shift from one state to another, be any simpler for our selves than it is for our bodies?

If we accept that relationships and interactions define self, what constitutes death of a self? Does the end of a body necessarily mean the end of self? What does it mean to die? In our lifetimes we end relationships, we shift group memberships, and people we know die. In each of these instances a little bit of us dies. To leave a group is to leave the part of the self defined by the group behind; the person you were in a relationship ceases to exist when the relationship ends. After your last class you're no longer a student. If your spouse dies, you're no longer a spouse but a widow. If you were a member of a church, but were excommunicated by the church, the part of you defined by the church community would be dead.

From this perspective, the body and the self live *and* die over time. When we describe self in terms of the physical body, the self wholly contained within our skin, physical death is the end of self. But when we allow for a social definition of self, it's worth asking what death is and what it tells us about the nature of self.

How do we decide when someone is dead? Does life end when the heart stops, when higher-order brain function ceases, when the part of the brain that controls basic bodily functions shuts down completely? Is a person dead if they can recover from one of these situations? What if we could completely shut down all your bodily functions, perhaps even separate your organs from your body, then at some point in the future put you back together and revive you? Would you have been dead?

That your body is not completely dead just after you've been declared so medically is an interesting situation. What do we mean by dead? It is certainly not that every part of your body ceases to function. Many of us would still consider ourselves alive if the only thing left functioning was our brain. Is this because our memory would be intact? Is it because we think we could still interact with the world? Even if we could still interact with the world, would we be the same person? Would you still be you?

If I replaced your body, the apparatus you use to engage the world, your experience of the world would change. Would this mean you are a different person? Imagine I replace a person's eyes and ears so that their visual and audio input changed. Maybe it's something as simple as eye surgery to correct nearsightedness, or it's something as large as a cochlear implant to affect a person's aural experience. In each case, I have affected the way the person experiences the world. But I'd guess that most people would see the person as an improved version of him or her self.

Maybe you have an easy answer to all these questions. You are your brain, or at least your neural patterns. There are people who certainly accept this view and are just waiting for the time when they can upload themselves into a computer and live forever. Let's put aside for a moment the obvious problem that an upload would be a duplicate, a separate entity from the original, not an extension of it. If I upload your consciousness and there is a little glitch, maybe something programmed as sweet tastes sour—are you still you? How much of you could be glitchy before you were no longer you? How much of you is defined by your glitchiness, or at least nonpredictability? Again, the line between life and death is not a bright one. All of these questions about death are about life. What you think it means to die tells you what you think *you* are.

. . .

HUMANS HAVE LONG SEARCHED FOR the fountain of youth, the secret that allows us to conquer physical death once and for all. Impermanence can be terrifying. It's easy to spend our time diverting our thoughts from the inevitable. We chase money or power, engage in petty squabbles, and generally avoid the reality of our impending demise. We entertain ourselves with tragedies and messy farce. We hide our anxiety under baggage we accumulate as we meander through life.[1]

The fear of death is a defining piece of human existence and stories we've told since the beginning of our time. Let's return to the *Epic of Gilgamesh*. When Enkidu dies, Gilgamesh is inconsolable. He mourns and stays with the body, until a maggot drops out of one of his friend's nostrils. The sign of decay shakes him and causes him to consider his own mortality. Here we have a vivid representation of physical mortality followed by a quest for immortality that ends fruitlessly. Despite these ancient poets' recognition of the folly of seeking immortality, the quest for never-ending life is a staple of human culture.

In 2019, scientists discovered a two-thousand-year-old bronze pot in a burial chamber in China that contained a yellowish liquid that smelled like wine. At first they thought it was liquor, but further analysis showed that the liquid contained potassium nitrate and alunite, a combination of chemicals that matched recipes for immortality elixirs described in Taoist texts from the time. While it's not known if the liquid discovered was ever consumed, there are numerous suspected cases of Chinese elites dying after ingesting elixirs intended to grant immortality.

We still haven't given up on the search for immortality; we've only turned to different methods. If you obtain membership in the Alcor Life Extension Foundation, after being declared dead you can have your body maintained at subfreezing temperatures with the hope that you can be reanimated when medical technology is capable of fixing what killed you. In an attempt at immortality that would not require you to die first, an entrepreneur, Dmitry Itskov, started the 2045 Initiative. According to the organization's website, the main science project "aims to create technologies enabling the transfer of an individual's personality to a more advanced non-biological carrier, and extending life, including to the point of immortality." In essence, he aims to create machines—we might call them robots or cyborgs—that can house and support a human's essence—probably understood to be the person's mind—without a human body, thereby extending life indefinitely.[2]

In both of these cases the goal appears to be the extension of the self as you know it today. Presumably reanimation would be akin to waking up after a particularly long sleep. You might be a little groggy, but you would still be you. In the case of the 2045 Initiative this is explicit. The aim is to transfer your personality to an infinitely upgradeable or repairable "non-biological carrier." My understanding, and I assume most others' as well, is that the "transfer of your personality" means that you would be the same you after the transfer.

Who knows, we just might produce the technology capable of freezing and reanimating people years after their cause of death has been cured. We might create enough computational sophistication and power to copy an individual's neural patterns and upload it to the cloud. But, if people succeeded in their quest for these versions of immortality, they might destroy what they fought so hard to save—success could be the end of their humanity, not the extension of it. This quest for immortality assumes that a person would be the same if they existed as pure consciousness, assuming such a thing even exists. Even if you could upload your consciousness to the cloud, you would still die, because the *you* in the cloud is fundamentally not *you*. You cannot exist without the social relationships, the social context that makes you *you*. To be the *you* you are now would require us to re-create the social circumstances in which you exist. The belief that we, creatures of imperfection embedded in a network of imperfect others, could persist absent our and their imperfections might be to misunderstand our present nature.

You could reanimate a body, without restarting the experience of a life you hoped to preserve. What we value in life, our intelligence or generosity or strength of spirit, might require something other than our consciousness. What we want, our continuation of our self as we experience it now, requires the social context that we currently live in.

AS WE AGE, WE ALL have an awareness of physical decline and with this some sense of loss—we are not today, as we've been. On the other hand, most of us are self-essentialists; our sense of self feels relatively stable. When we wake up tomorrow, we will be who we are today. Maybe the fear of physical decline elicits a fear for our selves that we can't quite comprehend. To say that you know you are going to die is one thing; to really understand it is something else. All we've ever experienced is life, all we know, is being. So maybe we seek to extend our physical experience, our sensual interface with the world, as a means of maintaining our selves.

Sure, the idea of physical death is unpleasant, but this isn't a fear of death so much as it's a fear of a process associated with life. The potential for pain, the loss of vitality, indignities that might be visited upon you by the medical establishment, these are all concerns associated with the process of death during life. In death, presumably your experience of all of this comes to an end. For this reason, it's not clear what there is to fear about *not being*, but *not being here* is a different situation.

If you believe that a version of your self lives on after your body, death means you're not here physically. This might elicit a fear of permanent separation from those you care about. It might also elicit fear of the unknown, of where you're going. These are fears of not being here or bereavement. Death could also mean true oblivion, not being. Here those left behind still have much to mourn, but what is there for the departed to fear? What would it even mean to fear the experience of oblivion? There would be no "you" to have that experience.

You certainly have your own beliefs about what comes after your body expires, if anything. As for me, I am not a believer in life after death, when life in this case means a continuation of my conscious experience. I don't believe that a form of my body or my unique consciousness will persist. But as should be clear by now, I don't think that these things constitute my self. The body and the self are linked, but they are not one and the same.

So, perhaps, a self can remain after the body dies. Rather than life after death, think of it as self after death. But the self is not immortal, either. Although the self can outlive the body, just as the body dies, eventually so does the self.

When my body dies, what will almost certainly depart is my conscious experience: enjoying a glass of wine, the air rushing by on a motorcycle ride, the experience of dancing with my partner. And so I try to savor every moment that moves me, as well as the more mundane ones, because these depend on a conscious interface with the world that I don't expect will outlive my body. When I am doing life right, I'm immersed in it, it's always there in an album, a conversation, a wonderful meal, a terrible meeting, a breeze through the trees. This I don't expect to persist.

What I do expect to persist to some degree is my socially constructed self. Meaning, I hope relationships I have made will sustain my self. For at least some period of time, new people might discover my experience of life and relate to me from their unique social situation. As a faculty member I've advised a number of PhD students, and maybe those students will tell their students about me. They'll likely make fun of my tendency to rant or they'll do impressions of my mannerisms in presentations. These new students might never meet me, but they would have some sense of what I was like, some inkling of how I influenced their advisors, and would have been influenced, in turn, by me. I would, in this way, participate in the future of academic study that I didn't have the chance to experience physically.

The claim that my self can exist after physical death is not meant to be mystical. I don't expect to live on as a conscious spirit, some ghost watching over people, although that might be cool. My hope is that my family and friends, the people I touch in some way, will maintain a relationship with their experience of me and engage with each other around their shared experience of me. I hope that they talk about the times we shared, they make fun of my foibles, and that these conversations serve to connect them to each other, and in so doing tighten their connection to my memory and to me. These interactions sustain my relationships that constitute my self now, and can persist after my body passes. What's left after we die are relationships. These relationships are not extinguished when the body dies. They may be transformed by grief and the divide between physical life and death, but relationships persist.

Something of my self is alive as long as I'm remembered. I'm not the only one to think this way. Lots of people talk about a legacy when they're gone. The very wealthy sometimes pay millions to have their names or the names of loved ones put on buildings. I teach at the Leland Stanford Junior University, which is named after the only child of the founding family, a boy who died at fifteen. The desire to be tied to something that persists, to leave something of the self behind seems to me a desire for an extension of self beyond death. Presumably, this book will continue on after I am dead. New people will read it and interact with me. Maybe they'll wiggle their fingers like I ask in the Introduction. By writing this book, I'm creating the possibility of connection between my self and selves of the future.

Imagine that my mother meets with a terrible accident and dies, but I don't know it. If death means the end of relationships, then my relationship with my mother would end the moment she died. Somehow that doesn't sound right. Maybe the relationship ends the moment I find out about her death. But that doesn't sound right, either. It could be that I carry that relationship with me to the end of my physical life. I could hear my mother's voice for the rest of my life, and it could shape the way I show up in a variety of relationships that my mother never knew. If you believe that my relationship with my mother persists beyond the moment of her death, then you understand why I say that physical death is not the end of self.

Let's go a step further. Assume I have a child and through me that child has a relationship with my mother. My child has a sense of my mother, her grandmother, albeit only through stories, photos, and videos. You could argue that my child has a relationship with her grandmother, even though she never met her in person. My child could feel pride in, want to emulate, want to impress, her grandmother. Thoughts of her grandmother could shape the way she interacts in relationships and the choices she makes about her future.

You might argue that my child wouldn't really know my mother, her grandmother. If by this you mean that my child would have no firsthand knowledge of her grandmother, you would be correct. But why does that matter? Presumably it matters because it means my daughter doesn't know enough about her grandmother, or she doesn't know my mother's *true* self. Do I really know my mother because I was raised by her?

What does it mean to really know someone? It almost certainly can't mean to know everything about the person. At some point, you've probably been surprised to learn something about someone you thought you knew incredibly well. Adding to the near impossibility of knowing everything about someone, your experience of a person is unique to you, because you are unique. Everything you know about a person is filtered through everything that is you.

You bring something to every relationship . . . your self. The way you experience others will be shared, but that doesn't mean that the person you know and the person I know are the same thing. You've certainly experienced this. Think of a time when you met the parents of a good friend for the first time. Often you see a "different side" of your friend. Maybe he is normally boisterous, but with his parents he is surprisingly mild-mannered. What you are really seeing is a different self, a self created by a different network of relationships than the network you typically see the person in.

You probably don't ask which self is real, the one I knew before or the one I see with my friend's parents: they are both real. The idea that my child has a different view of my mother doesn't mean that mine is the real one just because I knew my mother differently. In fact, it's possible that my child could tell me something about my mother that I didn't know but believe is true, because my child would have insight about her grand-mother through her understanding of me. Selves are as complex as the relationships that constitute them.

So, even if we think that relationships go in two directions—selves affecting each other—death doesn't preclude the pos-sibility of a real relationship, even with someone who maybe didn't know you in life. If self is a network of interactions and relationships, it exists as long as relationships that sustain it exist. Death isn't the end of relationships, and that means that physical death isn't the end of selves.

THE IDEA THAT THE SELF can outlive the body is not the same as the idea that the self is immortal. Selves exist in relationships; they live and evolve in interactions. As long as the constellation of relationships and interactions that produced your self continues to exist within the relationships and interactions of others, your self lives. Is it the same self that existed prior to your physical death? No. But are you the same self that you were yesterday?

If tomorrow everyone you ever knew forgot or denied your existence, your self would cease to exist—whether your body died or not. If everyone you ever knew died, and no newly born people knew of your existence, your self would also cease to exist. Eventually this fate will befall us all, but it is not physical death that marks the beginning or end of the process.

Our selves will grow old. Thoughts of our exploits will fade, memories of our zest for life will blur, the sharp edges of our desires will soften. This happens over a lifetime. Sometimes we treat the older among us as if they haven't experienced desire as intensely as we do, as if their rage never had the heat of ours, as if they weren't once as we are now. Memories of us and the relationships they sustain will evolve and eventually fade. This is the process of death of selves.

We might end with the idea that our selves, and the selves of our loved ones, can persist beyond physical death. But instead, I will end on a different note: we all die at least twice, once physically and another a more final death of self. Today, notwithstanding efforts at immortality, the best bet is that our bodies will die. We will be remembered for a time; our selves will persist. But eventually even memories of us that exist in relationships will fade and die as well. I don't think we can eradicate death, but maybe we shouldn't want to.

Physical death gives life heft and meaning. You appreciate life in part because it's finite. Each moment is a possibility; that they do not stretch out infinitely in front of you can motivate action as well as fear and resignation. You live well by choosing motivation and appreciation rather than resignation and fear. Death gives you the gift of limited possibility.

Death, when confronted, forces us to engage each other as the limited creatures we are. When we die we hope others mourn us. But perhaps we also create space for them to expand.

Who we were becomes part of their story; perhaps without the richness we brought, but also with less of the limitations we imposed. We bring unique experiences to relationships and shift the boundaries of our partners', our friends', our family members' selves. Our very presence makes others, and then makes demands. These relationships are what constitute a life. They can also produce an ethic: maybe we should strive to give generously and leave gracefully. No party does—nor should—last forever.

# Conclusion

I feel a deep sense of awe and wonder about the social nature of our existence. I still remember the feeling in graduate school of a new world opening before me as I encountered some of the ideas in this book. It felt like there was a world operating below the surface of the one I lived in, and now and then I could see the springs and gears that made the whole thing work. I clearly saw the human need for connection, the effect others have on the way we see the world, our need for order and our ability to fashion it collectively. There are worlds beneath the mundane interactions we have every day, but most of the time we only focus on what we need to get by.

For me, it's incredible to see the operation of our lives a little more clearly—the immense web of relationships that shape our existence—to see how much mystery there is to understand. But I've been told this isn't enough. Apparently, people want to know what to do with this information, how to navigate the world once the blinders are off. The truth is I don't think it's my place to tell you what you should do with it. Remember, I opened this book by telling you that there is no paint-by-numbers way to fix your life, and my goal isn't to fix your life anyway. Still, these ideas matter and can affect the way you think about your life and live. Let me clarify how.

I opened with an implicit promise to help you understand yourself and the way you came to be wherever you are in life. I've told you that your self is the product of a complex array of relationships and interactions. Said that way, I realize this idea might sound obvious. I hope it does. But what happens when you come to see and believe that your self is a social creation? The aim of this book has been to examine answers to that question.

If we are created by others, we can only be so free. I don't think this is a problem. In fact, I believe that the constraint of social structure is comforting. As we've seen, the idea of unlimited choice is less satisfying than you might imagine. More importantly, to engage effectively with others, to be understood, we need to be recognizable by others.

That relationships are necessary and yet curtail our freedom is the easy part. The harder thing to accept might be that your self is not an ineffable, unchanging thing imparted to you at birth. Yes, you are born with a biological blueprint (DNA), but this is not destiny. That there is no essential self in there to be discovered challenges the way people understand themselves, and we don't respond well to challenges to our worldview. What's important for us in all of this is the assumption that we know ourselves, that our sense of ourselves captures some enduring truth, something deeper than mere appearances that defines us. I've asked you to relax this view, to consider the possibility that your self is a dynamic product of your social world. I understand this is a big ask.

We do well when the world feels predictable, so the idea that you and I, the center of the world from our perspectives, are fluid might cause discomfort. If the center isn't stable, what else could be? To add insult to injury, in the world I've sketched no one can manifest their own reality. In this world, who you are and where you are—good and bad—is the product of people and social forces that you and I have only the barest sense of. Throughout your life and right now you are subject to all sorts of influences, and these influences have brought you to this point, and will take you wherever you go next. Of course, you already knew this, and yet . . .

We still cling to the idea that we are, or should be, firmly in the driver's seat. It would be hard to live without the feeling of freedom, the feeling that you are responsible for your life, the feeling that you are or could be in control of your destiny. Whether you have freedom or whether such freedom confers responsibility is important but beside my point. My point is that we often misunderstand the "I" we are so focused on. What I've offered is an alternative to the way most people understand their selves.

If we can choose who we are, we can never do so alone. The options you can imagine, your preferences, your reading of the consequences of your actions, the *actual* consequences of your actions are all tied to the social landscape you inhabit. We are mirrors—cut by biology, polished and shaped by relationships, made meaningful by culture—reflecting our reality to others.

MANY PEOPLE MIGHT NOT LIKE the implications of the views I've offered. If you live in comfort or enjoy significant social privileges, my arguments might be uncomfortable. Often, it's not enough to have good things in life; we need to see these things as evidence of our virtue rather than accidents of birth or social circumstances. Maybe that virtue manifests as work ethic, maybe it's innate intelligence, maybe it's the divine touch of noble birth. Whatever it is requires some essence to attach to. The absence of an essential, core self requires significant humility in the face of great success, and this is often hard to manage.

On the other side, if life is a struggle, things might be a bit more complicated, but there are still reasons to want a core self. The idea of a core separate from your circumstances allows you to imagine bending the world in a different direction. You can "get your head right," "get your hustle on," "start believing in yourself," or some other such self-admonishment to improve your situation. An essential self is separate from and can rise above what the world allots. You can overcome your circumstances.

Given the costs, why should you adopt my way of thinking? What do you get in return? My hope is that this way of thinking deepens your understanding of your and others' selves and adds another dimension to your experience of life. There is value in understanding the role you play in creating others. You exert influence on those around you. Your existence makes demands of others. There is power and responsibility in acknowledging and embracing this idea.

OFTEN, WE THINK OF POWER in terms of controlling resources that others want. I can promise you money or threaten you with some form of punishment. But if you accept that we create and shape each other, power doesn't require controlling material outcomes. You have power in mundane, everyday interactions. You affirm or challenge others' selves. You open or deny possibilities of being, and others do the same for you. What would change about the way you behave, about the world, if you and others took this possibility and the responsibility it entails seriously?

When we make decisions about who counts as a woman or man, Black or White, American or German, we are affecting who and what others can be. When we ask to be seen as women or men, Black or White, American or German, we are also asking others to (re)consider who they are. When you deny others the easy connection of a "Good morning!" or a simple smile of recognition, it affects both you and them. In those interactions you, for just a moment, deny them recognition of their humanity and you lose the opportunity to have yours affirmed as well.

Relationships and the communities they create are complicated affairs. We aren't born into empty worlds waiting for us to create them. We, and the relationships that constitute our selves, exist in communities—networks of selves—connected to the past and projected into the future.

There is nothing "natural" about the meaning wrapped around identities that tie us to communities of selves. You aren't just this or that identity. You are this or that identity in this or that community—one thing in one place, something else in another. Communities confer identities and this gives them tremendous power. It's a painful experience to live in a community that refuses to see you as you would like to be seen. But it is when the community has the *power* to enforce its view of reality that it becomes dangerous. Nation-states organize and run the world. International politics, national politics, even local politics often pit communities against one another. And selves in these communities are willing to fight, sometimes literally to the death, in the name of their group.

You can't truly understand politics without understanding that selves construct communities and communities provide the sense of immortality that selves crave. Any politician worth their salt knows that few things are more effective than rallying people around a shared identity, especially in reaction to a perceived enemy. The fight for identity is an existential struggle.

Our beliefs about the way selves work, what selves are, affect our experience of life: what you believe you are owed; what you think you should accomplish; what makes for a good life. These and numerous other beliefs affect the way you live and the way your life feels to you. Yet many of these beliefs rest on unexamined assumptions. What would it mean to believe you deserve more than others, if you also believed you were a creation of those other people? Maybe you'd ask yourself what best serves your community, knowing that it makes and remakes you every day?

If you're unhappy with an aspect of your self, the way of thinking I'm offering suggests you consider your relationships, rather than looking inward. How do you engage with those close to you? What do you produce in them and what do they in turn produce in you? What communities do you belong to? What social identities define you?

If your self is a social creation, so are others' selves. If we can see people this way, we might be able to reach a deeper state of equanimity. The ability to forgive or look past flaws in others might be a bit easier if we must all take credit. Just like ours, their selves are the result of their relationships.

Maybe you live with more kindness, patience, and generosity. Maybe life is just a little easier to bear and others just a bit easier to understand.

# Notes

## Introduction: You'll Be My Mirror

1. Gilbert, Daniel T., Elizabeth C. Pinel, Timothy D. Wilson, Stephen J. Blumberg, and Thalia P. Wheatley. "Immune Neglect: A Source of Durability Bias in Affective Forecasting." *Journal of Personality and Social Psychology* 75, no. 3 (1998): 617–38. https://doi.org/10.1037/0022–3514.75.3.617.

2. Wilson, T. D. *Strangers to Ourselves: Discovering the Adaptive Unconscious.* Cambridge, MA: Belknap Press of Harvard University Press, 2002.

3. Wilson, T. D., and D. T. Gilbert. "Affective forecasting: Knowing what to want." *Current Directions in Psychological Science*, 2005.

4. Wilson, Timothy D., Thalia Wheatley, Jonathan M. Meyers, Daniel T. Gilbert, and Danny Axsom. "Focalism: A Source of Durability Bias in Affective Forecasting." *Journal of Personality and Social Psychology* 78, no. 5 (2000): 821–36. https://doi.org/10.1037/0022–3514.78.5.821.

5. Hoffman, Donald. *The Case against Reality: Why Evolution Hid the Truth from Our Eyes.* New York: Norton, 2019.

6. Mezulis, Amy H., Lyn Y. Abramson, Janet S. Hyde, and Benjamin L. Hankin. "Is there a universal positivity bias in attributions? A meta-analytic review of individual, developmental, and cultural differences in the self-serving attributional bias." *Psychological Bulletin* 130, no. 5 (2004): 711.

7. Sloman, S. A., and P. Fernbach. *The Knowledge Illusion: Why We Never Think Alone.* New York: Penguin, 2018, pp. 296–98.

8. Gigerenzer, Gerd, and Daniel G. Goldstein. "Reasoning the Fast and Frugal Way: Models of Bounded Rationality." *Psychological Review* 103, no. 4 (1996): 650–69. https://doi.org/10.1037/0033–295x.103.4.650.

9. Kahneman, Daniel. "A Perspective on Judgment and Choice: Mapping Bounded Rationality." *American Psychologist* 58, no. 9 (2003): 697–720.

10. Cooley, Charles Horton. "Looking-glass self." *The Production of Reality: Essays and Readings on Social Interaction* 6 (1902): 126–28.

11. Mead, George Herbert, and Cornelius Schubert. *Mind, Self and Society* 111. Chicago: University of Chicago Press, 1934.

12. Gaither, Sarah E., Samantha P. Fan, and Katherine D. Kinzler. "Thinking about Multiple Identities Boosts Children's Flexible Thinking." *Developmental Science* 23, no. 1 (July 2, 2019). https://doi.org/10.1111/desc.12871.

13. Suh, Eunkook M. "Culture, Identity Consistency, and Subjective Well-Being." *Journal of Personality and Social Psychology* 83, no. 6 (2002): 1378–91. https://doi.org/10.1037/0022–3514.83.6.1378.

14. Steele, Claude M. *Whistling Vivaldi: How Stereotypes Affect Us and What We Can Do.* New York: Norton, 2011.

15. Gibson, Carolyn E., Joy Losee, and Christine Vitiello. "A Replication Attempt of Stereotype Susceptibility." *Social Psychology* 45, no. 3 (May 2014): 194–98. https://doi.org/10.1027/1864–9335/a000184.

16. Shih, Margaret, Todd L. Pittinsky, and Nalini Ambady. "Stereotype Susceptibility: Identity Salience and Shifts in Quantitative Performance." *Psychological Science* 10, no. 1 (January 1999): 80–83. https://doi.org/10.1111/1467–9280.00111.

17. Shih, Margaret, Todd L. Pittinsky, and Amy Trahan. "Domain-Specific Effects of Stereotypes on Performance." *Self and Identity* 5, no. 1 (January 2006): 1–14. https://doi.org/10.1080/15298860500338534.

18. Carse, James P. *Finite and Infinite Games: A Vision of Life as Play and Possibility.* New York: Free Press, 2012.

19. Maier, Steven F., and Martin E. Seligman. "Learned helplessness: Theory and evidence." *Journal of Experimental Psychology: General* 105, no. 1 (1976): 3.

20. Kay, Aaron C., Jennifer A. Whitson, Danielle Gaucher, and Adam D. Galinsky. "Compensatory Control." *Current Directions in Psychological Science* 18, no. 5 (October 2009): 264–68. https://doi.org/10.1111/j.1467–8721.2009.01649.x.

21. Landau, Mark J., Aaron C. Kay, and Jennifer A. Whitson. "Compensatory Control and the Appeal of a Structured World." *Psychological Bulletin* 141, no. 3 (May 2015): 694–722. https://doi.org/10.1037/a0038703.

22. Marsh, Abigail A., Hillary Anger Elfenbein, and Nalini Ambady. "Nonverbal 'Accents': Cultural Differences in Facial Expressions

of Emotion." *Psychological Science* 14, no. 4 (July 2003): 373–76.
https://doi.org/10.1111/1467–9280.24461.

23. Swann, William B., Alan Stein-Seroussi, and R. Brian Giesler.
"Why People Self-Verify." *Journal of Personality and Social
Psychology* 62, no. 3 (1992): 392–401. https://doi.org/10
.1037/0022–3514.62.3.392.

24. Stryker, Sheldon, and Peter J. Burke. "The Past, Present, and
Future of an Identity Theory." *Social Psychology Quarterly* 63, no. 4
(December 2000): 284. https://doi.org/10.2307/2695840.

## 1: The Search for Self

1. Borges, Jorge Luis. *Selected Non-Fictions: Volume 3.* New York:
Penguin Books, 2000.

2. Hume, David. *A Treatise of Human Nature.* Mineola, NY: Dover,
2003.

3. Rothbart, Mary K., Stephan A. Ahadi, Karen L. Hershey, and
Phillip Fisher. "Investigations of Temperament at Three to Seven
Years: The Children's Behavior Questionnaire." *Child Development*
72, no. 5 (September 2001): 1394–1408. https://doi.org/10
.1111/1467–8624.00355.

4. Rothbart, Mary K., Stephan A. Ahadi, and David E. Evans.
"Temperament and Personality: Origins and Outcomes." *Journal of
Personality and Social Psychology* 78, no. 1 (2000): 122–35. https://
doi.org/10.1037/0022–3514.78.1.122.

5. Roberts, Brent W., and Wendy F. DelVecchio. "The Rank-Order
Consistency of Personality Traits from Childhood to Old Age: A
Quantitative Review of Longitudinal Studies." *Psychological Bulletin*
126, no. 1 (2000): 3–25. https://doi.org/10.1037/0033–2909.126
.1.3.

6. Strohminger, Nina, and Shaun Nichols. "The Essential Moral Self."
*Cognition* 131, no. 1 (April 2014): 159–71. https://doi.org/10.1016/j
.cognition.2013.12.005.

7. Ross, Lee, and Andrew Ward. "Naive realism in everyday life:
Implications for social conflict and misunderstanding." *Values and
Knowledge* (1996): 103–35.

8. Echterhoff, Gerald, E. Tory Higgins, and John M. Levine. "Shared
Reality: Experiencing Commonality with Others' Inner States
about the World." *Perspectives on Psychological Science* 4, no. 5
(September 2009): 496–521. https://doi.org/10.1111/j.1745–6924
.2009.01161.x.

9. Higgins, E. Tory, Maya Rossignac-Milon, and Gerald Echterhoff.
"Shared Reality: From Sharing Is Believing to Merging Minds."

*Current Directions in Psychological Science* 30, no. 2 (April 2021): 103–10. https://doi.org/10.1177/0963721421992027.

10. Allport, Gordon W. *The Nature of Prejudice*. Boston: Addison-Wesley, 1954.

11. Friesen, Justin P., Aaron C. Kay, Richard P. Eibach, and Adam D. Galinsky. "Seeking Structure in Social Organization: Compensatory Control and the Psychological Advantages of Hierarchy." *Journal of Personality and Social Psychology* 106, no. 4 (2014): 590–609. https://doi.org/10.1037/a0035620.

12. Whitson, J. A., and A. D. Galinsky. "Lacking Control Increases Illusory Pattern Perception." *Science* 322, no. 5898 (October 3, 2008): 115–17. https://doi.org/10.1126/science.1159845.

13. Hoffman, Donald. *The Case against Reality: Why Evolution Hid the Truth from Our Eyes*. New York: Norton, 2019.

14. Koffka, K. *Principles of Gestalt Psychology*. New York: Harcourt, Brace, 1935.

15. Richer, P. "The concepts of subjectivity and objectivity in Gestalt psychology." *Journal of Phenomenological Psychology* 10, no. 1 (1979).

16. Bechlivanidis, Christos, Marc J. Buehner, Emma C. Tecwyn, David A. Lagnado, Christoph Hoerl, and Teresa McCormack. "Human Vision Reconstructs Time to Satisfy Causal Constraints." *Psychological Science* 33, no. 2 (January 4, 2022): 224–35. https://doi.org/10.1177/09567976211032663.

17. Whitson, Jennifer A., Adam D. Galinsky, and Aaron Kay. "The Emotional Roots of Conspiratorial Perceptions, System Justification, and Belief in the Paranormal." *Journal of Experimental Social Psychology* 56 (January 2015): 89–95. https://doi.org/10.1016/j.jesp.2014.09.002.

18. Macrae, C. Neil, Alan B. Milne, and Galen V. Bodenhausen. "Stereotypes as Energy-Saving Devices: A Peek inside the Cognitive Toolbox." *Journal of Personality and Social Psychology* 66, no. 1 (January 1994): 37–47. https://doi.org/10.1037/0022-3514.66.1.37.

19. J. Aislinn Bohren, Kareem Haggag, Alex Imas, Devin G. Pope, and National Bureau. *Inaccurate Statistical Discrimination: An Identification Problem*. Cambridge, MA: National Bureau of Economic Research, 2019.

20. Fiske, Susan T., and Shelley E. Taylor. *Social Cognition: From Brains to Culture*. Thousand Oaks, CA: SAGE, 2013.

21. Laurin, Kristin, Aaron C. Kay, and David A. Moscovitch. "On the Belief in God: Towards an Understanding of the Emotional Substrates of Compensatory Control." *Journal of Experimental*

*Social Psychology* 44, no. 6 (November 2008): 1559–62. https://doi
.org/10.1016/j.jesp.2008.07.007.

22. Goldstein, Noah J., Robert B. Cialdini, and Vladas Griskevicius.
"A Room with a Viewpoint: Using Social Norms to Motivate
Environmental Conservation in Hotels." *Journal of Consumer
Research* 35, no. 3 (October 2008): 472–82. https://doi.org/10
.1086/586910.

23. Armel, K. Carrie, and V. S. Ramachandran. "Projecting Sensations
to External Objects: Evidence from Skin Conductance Response."
*Proceedings of the Royal Society of London. Series B: Biological
Sciences* 270, no. 1523 (July 22, 2003): 1499–1506. https://doi.org
/10.1098/rspb.2003.2364.

24. Porciello, Giuseppina, Ilaria Bufalari, Ilaria Minio-Paluello, Enrico
Di Pace, and Salvatore Maria Aglioti. "The 'Enfacement' Illusion:
A Window on the Plasticity of the Self." *Cortex* 104 (July 2018):
261–75. https://doi.org/10.1016/j.cortex.2018.01.007.

25. Sforza, Anna, Ilaria Bufalari, Patrick Haggard, and Salvatore
M. Aglioti. "My Face in Yours: Visuo-Tactile Facial Stimulation
Influences Sense of Identity." *Social Neuroscience* 5, no. 2 (April
2010): 148–62. https://doi.org/10.1080/17470910903205503.

26. Langlois, Judith H., Jean M. Ritter, Rita J. Casey, and Douglas
B. Sawin. "Infant Attractiveness Predicts Maternal Behaviors
and Attitudes." *Developmental Psychology* 31, no. 3 (May 1995):
464–72. https://doi.org/10.1037/0012-1649.31.3.464.

27. Lorenzo, Genevieve L., Jeremy C. Biesanz, and Lauren J. Human.
"What Is Beautiful Is Good and More Accurately Understood."
*Psychological Science* 21, no. 12 (November 4, 2010): 1777–82.
https://doi.org/10.1177/0956797610388048.

28. Sherman, G. D., and P. H. Mehta. "Stress, Cortisol, and Social
Hierarchy." *Current Opinion in Psychology* 33 (June 1, 2020):
227–32. https://doi.org/10.1016/j.copsyc.2019.09.013.

29. Rueden, C. R. von, B. C. Trumble, M. Emery Thompson,
J. Stieglitz, P. L. Hooper, A. D. Blackwell, H. S. Kaplan, and
M. Gurven. "Political Influence Associates with Cortisol and
Health among Egalitarian Forager-Farmers." *Evolution, Medicine,
and Public Health*, no. 1 (September 11, 2014): 122–33. https://doi
.org/10.1093/emph/eou021.

30. Chetty, Raj, John N. Friedman, Nathaniel Hendren, Maggie R.
Jones, and Sonya R. Porter. *The Opportunity Atlas: Mapping the
Childhood Roots of Social Mobility*, no. w25147. Cambridge, MA:
National Bureau of Economic Research, 2018.

31. Chetty, Raj, Nathaniel Hendren, and National Bureau. *The Impacts
of Neighborhoods on Intergenerational Mobility I: Childhood Exposure*

*Effects.* Cambridge, MA: National Bureau of Economic Research, 2016.

## 2: False Promises

1. La Ferla, Ruth. "Manifesting for the Rest of Us." *New York Times,* January 23, 2021. https://www.nytimes.com/2021/01/20/style/self -care/how-to-manifest-2021.html.
2. Gill, Christopher. *The Structured Self in Hellenistic and Roman Thought.* Oxford: Oxford University Press, 2006.
3. Weintraub, Karl Joachim. *The Value of the Individual: Self and Circumstance in Autobiography.* Chicago and London: University of Chicago Press, 1982.
4. Siedentop, Larry. *Inventing the Individual: The Origins of Western Liberalism.* Cambridge, MA: Belknap Press of Harvard University Press, 2017.
5. Christy, Andrew G., Rebecca J. Schlegel, and Andrei Cimpian. "Why Do People Believe in a 'True Self'? The Role of Essentialist Reasoning about Personal Identity and the Self." *Journal of Personality and Social Psychology* 117, no. 2 (August 2019): 386–416. https://doi.org/10.1037/pspp0000254.
6. Schlegel, Rebecca J., and Joshua A. Hicks. "The True Self and Psychological Health: Emerging Evidence and Future Directions." *Social and Personality Psychology Compass* 5, no. 12 (December 2011): 989–1003. https://doi.org/10.1111/j.1751-9004.2011. 00401.x.
7. Strohminger, Nina, Joshua Knobe, and George Newman. "The True Self: A Psychological Concept Distinct from the Self." *Perspectives on Psychological Science* 12, no. 4 (July 2017): 551–60. https://doi .org/10.1177/1745691616689495.
8. Dulaney, Ellen S., Verena Graupmann, and Kimberly A. Quinn. "Who Am I and How Often? Variation in Self-Essentialism Beliefs, Cognitive Style, and Well-Being." *Personality and Individual Differences* 136 (January 2019): 148–59. https://doi.org/10.1016/j .paid.2017.10.011.
9. Mayr, Ulrich, and Alexandra M. Freund. "Do we become more prosocial as we age, and if so, why?" *Current Directions in Psychological Science* 29, no. 3 (2020): 248–54.
10. Taylor, Charles. *Sources of the Self: The Making of the Modern Identity.* Cambridge, MA: Harvard University Press, 1989.
11. Panofsky, Erwin. *Idea; a Concept in Art Theory.* Translated by Joseph J. S. Peake. Columbia, SC: University of South Carolina Press, 1968.

12. Descartes, René. *Discourse on Method and Meditations on First Philosophy.* Indianapolis, IN: Hackett, 1999.

13. Smith, Norman Kemp. *Immanuel Kant's Critique of Pure Reason.* Redditch, Great Britain: Read Books, 2011.

14. Smith, Adam. *An Inquiry into the Nature and Causes of the Wealth of Nations.* Petersfield, UK: Harriman House, 2010.

15. Smith, Adam. *The Theory of Moral Sentiments.* New York: Penguin, 2010.

16. Samuelson, Paul Anthony. *Economics: An Introductory Analysis.* New York: McGraw-Hill, 1997.

17. Adam, Hajo, Otilia Obodaru, and Adam D. Galinsky. "Who You Are Is Where You Are: Antecedents and Consequences of Locating the Self in the Brain or the Heart." *Organizational Behavior and Human Decision Processes* 128 (May 2015): 74–83. https://doi.org/10.1016/j.obhdp.2015.03.004.

18. Goldstein, M. "The Decade of the Brain." *Neurology* 40, no. 2 (1990): 321.

19. Bigenwald, Ariane, and Valerian Chambon. "Criminal Responsibility and Neuroscience: No Revolution Yet." *Frontiers in Psychology* 10 (June 27, 2019). https://doi.org/10.3389/fpsyg.2019.01406.

20. Serra, Daniel. "Decision-Making: From Neuroscience to Neuroeconomics—an Overview." *Theory and Decision* 91, no. 1 (June 2021). https://doi.org/10.1007/s11238–021–09830–3.

21. Cave, Stephen. *Immortality: The Quest to Live Forever and How It Drives Civilisation.* London: Biteback, 2013.

22. 2045.com. "2045 Initiative." Accessed July 6, 2022. http://2045.com/.

23. Wilson, Timothy D. *Strangers to Ourselves.* Cambridge, MA: Harvard University Press, 2004.

24. Lewicki, Pawel, Maria Czyzewska, and Hunter Hoffman. "Unconscious Acquisition of Complex Procedural Knowledge." *Journal of Experimental Psychology: Learning, Memory, and Cognition* 13, no. 4 (1987): 523–30. https://doi.org/10.1037/0278–7393.13.4.523.

25. Stadler, Michael A. "On Learning Complex Procedural Knowledge." *Journal of Experimental Psychology: Learning, Memory, and Cognition* 15, no. 6 (1989): 1061–69. https://doi.org/10.1037/0278–7393.15.6.1061.

26. Hume, David. *A Treatise of Human Nature.* Mineola, NY: Dover, 2003.

27. Schacter, Daniel L., Kenneth A. Norman, and Wilma Koutstaal. "The Cognitive Neuroscience of Constructive Memory." *Annual*

*Review of Psychology* 49, no. 1 (February 1998): 289–318. https://doi.org/10.1146/annurev.psych.49.1.289.

28. Zacks, Jeffrey M., Matthew A. Bezdek, and Garrett E. Cunningham. "Knowledge and the Reliability of Constructive Memory." *Memory* 30, no. 1 (January 2021): 1–4. https://doi.org/10.1080/09658211.2020.1871022.

29. Cohen, Lizabeth. "A Consumers' Republic: The Politics of Mass Consumption in Postwar America." *Journal of Consumer Research* 31, no. 1 (2004): 236–39. https://doi.org/10.1086/383439.

30. McWilliams, John C. *The 1960s Cultural Revolution: A Reference Guide*. Santa Barbara, CA: ABC-CLIO, 2020.

31. Kripal, Jeffrey J. *Esalen: America and the Religion of No Religion*. Chicago: University of Chicago Press, 2008.

32. Emerson, Ralph Waldo. *The Essential Writings of Ralph Waldo Emerson*. New York: Modern Library, 2000.

33. Rousseau, Jean-Jacques. *The Social Contract and Other Later Political Writings*. Cambridge: Cambridge University Press, 2018.

34. Berlin, Isaiah. *The Crooked Timber of Humanity: Chapters in the History of Ideas*. Princeton, NJ: Princeton University Press, 2013.

35. Berlin, Isaiah, and Henry Hardy. *Freedom and Its Betrayal: Six Enemies of Human Liberty*. Princeton, NJ: Princeton University Press, 2014.

36. Aquino, Karl, and Americus Reed. "The Self-Importance of Moral Identity." *Journal of Personality and Social Psychology* 83, no. 6 (2002): 1423–40. https://doi.org/10.1037/0022-3514.83.6.1423.

37. De Freitas, Julian, Mina Cikara, Igor Grossmann, and Rebecca Schlegel. "Moral Goodness Is the Essence of Personal Identity." *Trends in Cognitive Sciences* 22, no. 9 (September 2018): 739–40. https://doi.org/10.1016/j.tics.2018.05.006.

38. De Freitas, Julian, and Mina Cikara. "Deep Down My Enemy Is Good: Thinking about the True Self Reduces Intergroup Bias." *Journal of Experimental Social Psychology* 74 (January 2018): 307–16. https://doi.org/10.1016/j.jesp.2017.10.006.

39. Haslam, Nick. "Dehumanization: An integrative review." *Personality and Social Psychology Review* 10, no. 3 (2006): 252–64.

40. Bastian, Brock, and Nick Haslam. "Excluded from Humanity: The Dehumanizing Effects of Social Ostracism." *Journal of Experimental Social Psychology* 46, no. 1 (January 2010): 107–13.

41. Bastian, Brock, and Nick Haslam. "Experiencing Dehumanization: Cognitive and Emotional Effects of Everyday Dehumanization." *Basic and Applied Social Psychology* 33, no. 4 (October 2011): 295–303. https://doi.org/10.1080/01973533.2011.614132.

### 3: Freedom, Really?

1. MacCallum, Gerald C. "Negative and Positive Freedom." *Philosophical Review* 76, no. 3 (July 1967): 312–34. https://doi .org/10.2307/2183622.

2. American Civil Liberties Union of New York. "Stop-and-Frisk in the De Blasio Era (2019)." Accessed July 7, 2022. https://www .nyclu.org/en/publications/stop-and-frisk-de-blasio-era-2019.

3. Sidanius, Jim, and Felicia Pratto. *Social Dominance: An Intergroup Theory of Social Hierarchy and Oppression.* Cambridge: Cambridge University Press, 1999.

4. Raven, Bertram H. "The Bases of Power and the Power/Interaction Model of Interpersonal Influence." *Analyses of Social Issues and Public Policy* 8, no. 1 (September 15, 2008): 1–22. https://doi.org /10.1111/j.1530–2415.2008.00159.x.

5. Pelley, Virginia. "Love Has Lost." *Marie Claire*, September 7, 2021. https://www.marieclaire.com/culture/a37417778/love-has-won -cult-amy-carlson-stroud-death/.

6. Moyer, Christopher. "From 'Mother God' to Mummified Corpse: Inside the Fringe Spiritual Sect 'Love Has Won.'" *Rolling Stone*, November 26, 2021. https://www.rollingstone.com/culture /culture-features/love-has-won-amy-carlson-mother-god-1254916/.

7. Young, Harvey. "The Black Body as Souvenir in American Lynching." *Theatre Journal* 57, no.4 (2005): 639–57. https://doi.org /10.1353/tj.2006.0054.

8. Wengrow, David. *The Dawn of Everything: A New History of Humanity.* London: Allen Lane, 2021.

9. Young, Harvey. "The Black Body as Souvenir in American Lynching." *Theatre Journal* 57, no. 4 (2005): 639–57. https://doi.org /10.1353/tj.2006.0054.

10. Christy, Andrew G., Elizabeth Seto, Rebecca J. Schlegel, Matthew Vess, and Joshua A. Hicks. "Straying from the Righteous Path and from Ourselves." *Personality and Social Psychology Bulletin* 42, no. 11 (September 28, 2016): 1538–50. https://doi.org/10.1177 /0146167216665095.

11. Ochs, Elinor, and Lisa Capps. "Narrating the Self." *Annual Review of Anthropology* 25, no. 1 (October 21, 1996): 19–43. https://doi.org /10.1146/annurev.anthro.25.1.19.

12. Berent, Iris, and Melanie Platt. "The True 'Me'—Mind or Body?" *Journal of Experimental Social Psychology* 93 (March 2021): 104100. https://doi.org/10.1016/j.jesp.2020.104100.

13. Engs, Ruth, and David J. Hanson. "Reactance Theory: A Test with Collegiate Drinking." *Psychological Reports* 64, no. 3_suppl (June

1989): 1083–86. https://doi.org/10.2466/pr0.1989.64.3c
.1083.

## 4: Hugs and Straitjackets

1. Bastian, Brock, and Nick Haslam. "Excluded from humanity: The dehumanizing effects of social ostracism." *Journal of Experimental Social Psychology* 46, no. 1 (2010): 107–13.
2. Williams, Kipling D., Christopher K. T. Cheung, and Wilma Choi. "Cyberostracism: Effects of Being Ignored over the Internet." *Journal of Personality and Social Psychology* 79, no. 5 (2000): 748–62. https://doi.org/10.1037/0022–3514.79.5.748.
3. Higgins, E. Tory, Maya Rossignac-Milon, and Gerald Echterhoff. "Shared reality: From sharing-is-believing to merging minds." *Current Directions in Psychological Science* 30, no. 2 (2021): 103–10.
4. Tiedens, Larissa Z., and Alison R. Fragale. "Power Moves: Complementarity in Dominant and Submissive Nonverbal Behavior." *Journal of Personality and Social Psychology* 84, no. 3 (2003): 558–68. https://doi.org/10.1037/0022–3514.84.3.558.
5. Baaren, Rick B. van, William W. Maddux, Tanya L. Chartrand, Cris de Bouter, and Ad van Knippenberg. "It Takes Two to Mimic: Behavioral Consequences of Self-Construals." *Journal of Personality and Social Psychology* 84, no. 5 (2003): 1093–1102. https://doi.org/10.1037/0022–3514.84.5.1093.
6. Chartrand, Tanya L., and Jessica L. Lakin. "The Antecedents and Consequences of Human Behavioral Mimicry." *Annual Review of Psychology* 64, no. 1 (January 3, 2013): 285–308. https://doi.org/10.1146/annurev-psych-113011–143754.
7. Lowery, Brian S., Curtis D. Hardin, and Stacey Sinclair. "Social Influence Effects on Automatic Racial Prejudice." *Journal of Personality and Social Psychology* 81, no. 5 (2001): 842–55. https://doi.org/10.1037/0022–3514.81.5.842.
8. Rossignac-Milon, Maya, and E. Tory Higgins. "Epistemic Companions: Shared Reality Development in Close Relationships." *Current Opinion in Psychology* 23 (October 2018): 66–71. https://doi.org/10.1016/j.copsyc.2018.01.001.
9. Echterhoff, Gerald, E. Tory Higgins, and Stephan Groll. "Audience-Tuning Effects on Memory: The Role of Shared Reality." *Journal of Personality and Social Psychology* 89, no. 3 (2005): 257–76. https://doi.org/10.1037/0022–3514.89.3.257.
10. Chartrand, Tanya L., Amy N. Dalton, and Gavan J. Fitzsimons. "Nonconscious Relationship Reactance: When Significant Others

Prime Opposing Goals." *Journal of Experimental Social Psychology* 43, no. 5 (September 2007): 719–26. https://doi.org/10.1016/j.jesp .2006.08.003.

## 5: Building Selves

1. Aron, Arthur, Elaine N. Aron, Michael Tudor, and Greg Nelson. "Close Relationships as Including Other in the Self." *Journal of Personality and Social Psychology* 60, no. 2 (1991): 241–53. https:// doi.org/10.1037/0022–3514.60.2.241.
2. Aron, A., et al. "Including Close Others in the Cognitive Structure of the Self." In *Interpersonal Cognition* (New York: Guilford Press, 2005), pp. 206–32.
3. Aron, Arthur, Tracy McLaughlin-Volpe, Debra Mashek, Gary Lewandowski, Stephen C. Wright, and Elaine N. Aron. "Including Others in the Self." *European Review of Social Psychology* 15, no. 1 (January 2004): 101–32. https://doi.org/10 .1080/10463280440000008.
4. Pollack, Eileen. *The Only Woman in the Room: Why Science Is Still a Boys' Club.* Boston: Beacon, 2016.
5. Chartrand, Tanya L., Amy N. Dalton, and Gavan J. Fitzsimons. "Nonconscious relationship reactance: When significant others prime opposing goals." *Journal of Experimental Social Psychology* 43, no. 5 (2007): 719–26.
6. Hardin, Curtis D., and E. Tory Higgins. "Shared reality: How social verification makes the subjective objective." (1996).
7. Sherif, M. "A Study of Some Social Factors in Perception." *Archives of Psychology* 187, no. 60 (1935).
8. Sinclair, Stacey, Elizabeth Dunn, and Brian Lowery. "The Relationship between Parental Racial Attitudes and Children's Implicit Prejudice." *Journal of Experimental Social Psychology* 41, no. 3 (May 2005): 283–89. https://doi.org/10.1016/j.jesp.2004.06.003.
9. Tesser, A. "Toward a self-evaluation maintenance model of social behavior." *Advances in Experimental Social Psychology* 21 (1988): 181–227.
10. Festinger, Leon. "A Theory of Social Comparison Processes." *Human Relations* 7, no. 2 (1954): 117–40. https://doi.org/10.1177 /001872675400700202.
11. Eibach, Richard P., and Steven E. Mock. "Idealizing Parenthood to Rationalize Parental Investments." *Psychological Science* 22, no. 2 (January 18, 2011): 203–8. https://doi.org/10.1177/095679761 0397057.

## 6: I Am Because We Are

1. Brewer, Marilynn B., and Wendi Gardner. "Who Is This 'We'? Levels of Collective Identity and Self Representations." *Journal of Personality and Social Psychology* 71, no. 1 (1996): 83–93. https://doi.org/10.1037/0022–3514.71.1.83.

2. Hogg, Michael A., and Mark J. Rinella. "Social Identities and Shared Realities." *Current Opinion in Psychology* 23 (October 2018): 6–10. https://doi.org/10.1016/j.copsyc.2017.10.003.

3. Hogg, M. A. "Uncertainty-identity theory." *Advances in Experimental Social Psychology* 39 (2007): 69–126.

4. Iyengar, Shanto, Yphtach Lelkes, Matthew Levendusky, Neil Malhotra, and Sean J. Westwood. "The Origins and Consequences of Affective Polarization in the United States." *Annual Review of Political Science* 22, no. 1 (December 10, 2018). https://doi.org/10.1146/annurev-polisci-051117–073034.

5. Wilkerson, Isabel. *Caste: The Origins of Our Discontents.* Random House: NY, 2020.

6. *PARENTS INVOLVED IN COMMUNITY SCHOOLS v. SEATTLE SCHOOL DIST. NO. 1.* 551 U.S. 701 (2007).

7. McPherson, Miller, Lynn Smith-Lovin, and James M. Cook. "Birds of a Feather: Homophily in Social Networks." *Annual Review of Sociology* 27, no. 1 (August 2001): 415–44. https://doi.org/10.1146/annurev.soc.27.1.415.

8. Taylor, Shelley E., Susan T. Fiske, Nancy L. Etcoff, and Audrey J. Ruderman. "Categorical and Contextual Bases of Person Memory and Stereotyping." *Journal of Personality and Social Psychology* 36, no. 7 (1978): 778–93. https://doi.org/10.1037/0022–3514.36.7.778.

9. Fiske, S. T., and S. L. Neuberg. "A Continuum of Impression Formation, from Category-Based to Individuating Processes: Influences of Information and Motivation on Attention and Interpretation." *Advances in Experimental Social Psychology* 23 (1990).

10. Haslam, Nick, Louis Rothschild, and Donald Ernst. "Essentialist beliefs about social categories." *British Journal of Social Psychology* 39, no. 1 (2000): 113–27.

11. Prentice, Deborah A., and Dale T. Miller. "Psychological essentialism of human categories." *Current Directions in Psychological Science* 16, no. 4 (2007): 202–6.

12. Byrd, W. Carson, and Victor E. Ray. "Ultimate Attribution in the Genetic Era." *The Annals of the American Academy of Political and Social Science* 661, no. 1 (August 10, 2015): 212–35. https://doi.org/10.1177/0002716215587887.

13. Hewstone, Miles. "The 'Ultimate Attribution Error'? A Review of the Literature on Intergroup Causal Attribution." *European Journal of Social Psychology* 20, no. 4 (July 1990): 311–35. https://doi.org /10.1002/ejsp.2420200404.
14. Bolland, O. Nigel, and Orlando Patterson. "Slavery and Social Death: A Comparative Study." *Ethnohistory* 33, no. 2 (1986): 248. https://doi.org/10.2307/481796.
15. Harth, Nicole Syringa, Thomas Kessler, and Colin Wayne Leach. "Advantaged Group's Emotional Reactions to Intergroup Inequality: The Dynamics of Pride, Guilt, and Sympathy." *Personality and Social Psychology Bulletin* 34, no. 1 (January 2008): 115–29. https:// doi.org/10.1177/0146167207309193.
16. Welten, Stephanie C. M., Marcel Zeelenberg, and Seger M. Breugelmans. "Vicarious Shame." *Cognition & Emotion* 26, no. 5 (August 2012): 836–46. https://doi.org/10.1080/02699931.2011.6 25400.
17. Lickel, Brian, Toni Schmader, Mathew Curtis, Marchelle Scarnier, and Daniel R. Ames. "Vicarious Shame and Guilt." *Group Processes & Intergroup Relations* 8, no. 2 (April 2005): 145–57. https://doi.org /10.1177/1368430205051064.
18. Phillips, L. Taylor, and Brian S. Lowery. "The Hard-Knock Life? Whites Claim Hardships in Response to Racial Inequity." *Journal of Experimental Social Psychology* 61 (November 2015): 12–18. https:// doi.org/10.1016/j.jesp.2015.06.008.
19. Phillips, L. Taylor, and Brian S. Lowery. "I Ain't No Fortunate One: On the Motivated Denial of Class and Race Privilege." *Academy of Management Proceedings*, no. 1 (January 2015): 19158. https://doi .org/10.5465/ambpp.2015.19158abstract.
20. Harris, Cheryl I. "Whiteness as Property." *Harvard Law Review* 106, no. 8 (June 1993): 1707–91. https://doi.org/10.2307/1341787.
21. López, Ian Haney. *White by Law: The Legal Construction of Race.* New York: New York University Press, 2006.
22. Painter, Nell Irvin. *The History of White People.* New York: Norton, 2011.
23. Fry, Peter. "Politics, nationality, and the meanings of 'race' in Brazil." *Daedalus* 129, no. 2 (2000): 83–118.
24. Tilley, Chloe. "Halle Berry: 'My daughter is black.'" BBC, February 10, 2011. https://www.bbc.co.uk/blogs/worldhaveyoursay/2011/02 /halle_berry_my_daughter_is_bla.html.
25. Dolezal, Rachel, and Storms Reback. *In Full Color: Finding My Place in a Black and White World.* Dallas: Benbella Books, 2017.
26. St. Félix, Doreen "'The Rachel Divide' Review: A Disturbing Portrait of Dolezal's Racial Fraudulence." *New Yorker*, April 26, 2018.

27. Tuvel, Rebecca. "In Defense of Transracialism." *Hypatia* 32, no. 2 (March 29, 2017): 263–78. https://doi.org/10.1111/hypa .12327.

28. Mandalaywala, Tara M., Gabrielle Ranger-Murdock, David M. Amodio, and Marjorie Rhodes. "The Nature and Consequences of Essentialist Beliefs about Race in Early Childhood." *Child Development* 90, no. 4 (January 23, 2018): e437–53. https://doi .org/10.1111/cdev.13008.

29. Mancini, Olivia. "Passing as White: Anita Hemmings 1897." *Vassar: The Alumnae/i Quarterly* 98, no. 1 (Winter 2001). https://www .vassar.edu/vq/issues/2002/01/features/passing-as-white.html#: ~:text=%22She%20has%20a%20clear%20olive,pronounced%20 brunette%20of%20white%20race.%22.

30. Nelson, Maggie. *On Freedom: Four Songs of Care and Constraint.* London: Vintage Books, 2022.

31. Morrison, Toni. *Playing in the Dark: Whiteness and the Literary Imagination.* New York: Vintage, 1992.

32. Mailer, Norman. *The White Negro.* San Francisco: City Lights Books, 1972.

33. Gelman, S. "Psychological Essentialism in Children." *Trends in Cognitive Sciences* 8, no. 9 (September 2004): 404–9. https://doi .org/10.1016/j.tics.2004.07.001.

34. Medin, Douglas L., and Andrew Ortony. "Psychological essentialism." *Similarity and Analogical Reasoning* 179 (1989): 195.

35. "AncestryDNA Winter Sale," iSpot.tv, 0:28, published by AncestryDNA, February 8, 2018. https://www.ispot.tv/ad/weoJ /ancestrydna-winter-sale-greatness.

36. Gould, Stephen Jay. *The Mismeasure of Man.* New York: Norton, 1981.

37. Wu, Ellen D. "The color of success." In *The Color of Success.* Princeton, NJ: Princeton University Press, 2013.

38. Laqueur, Thomas. *Making Sex: Body and Gender from the Greeks to Freud.* Cambridge, MA: Harvard University Press, 1992.

39. Jackman, Mary R. *The Velvet Glove: Paternalism and Conflict in Gender, Class, and Race Relations.* Berkeley, CA: University of California Press, 1994.

40. Graham, Sandra, and Brian S. Lowery. "Priming unconscious racial stereotypes about adolescent offenders." *Law and Human Behavior* 28, no. 5 (2004): 483–504.

41. Rattan, Aneeta, Cynthia S. Levine, Carol S. Dweck, and Jennifer L. Eberhardt. "Race and the fragility of the legal distinction between juveniles and adults." *PLOS One* 7, no. 5 (2012): e36680.

42. Dolezal, Rachel, and Storms Reback. *In Full Color: Finding My Place in a Black and White World*. Dallas: Benbella Books, 2017.

43. Schmitt, Michael T., Russell Spears, and Nyla R. Branscombe. "Constructing a Minority Group Identity Out of Shared Rejection: The Case of International Students." *European Journal of Social Psychology* 33, no. 1 (January 2003): 1–12. https://doi.org/10.1002/ejsp.131.

44. Eshraghi, Adrien A., Ronen Nazarian, Fred F. Telischi, Suhrud M. Rajguru, Eric Truy, and Chhavi Gupta. "The Cochlear Implant: Historical Aspects and Future Prospects." *The Anatomical Record: Advances in Integrative Anatomy and Evolutionary Biology* 295, no. 11 (October 8, 2012): 1967–80. https://doi.org/10.1002/ar.22580.

45. AudismFreeAmerica. "NAD's 1991 Position Statement on Cochlear Implants." Blogspot.com, 2009. http://audismfreeamerica.blogspot.com/2009/06/nads-1991-position-statement-on.html.

46. Bourdieu, Pierre. *Outline of a Theory of Practice*. Cambridge: Cambridge University Press, 1977.

47. Appiah, Kwame Anthony. *Lies That Bind: Rethinking Identity*. New York: Liveright, 2019.

48. Bouterse, Leah, and Cara Wall-Scheffler. "Children are not like other loads: A cross-cultural perspective on the influence of burdens and companionship on human walking." *PeerJ* 6 (2018): e5547.

49. Wu, Peixia, Clyde C. Robinson, Chongming Yang, Craig H. Hart, Susanne F. Olsen, Christin L. Porter, Shenghua Jin, Jianzhong Wo, and Xinzi Wu. "Similarities and Differences in Mothers' Parenting of Preschoolers in China and the United States." *International Journal of Behavioral Development* 26, no. 6 (November 2002): 481–91. https://doi.org/10.1080/01650250143000436.

50. Jetten, Jolanda, Nyla R. Branscombe, S. Alexander Haslam, Catherine Haslam, Tegan Cruwys, Janelle M. Jones, Lijuan Cui, et al. "Having a Lot of a Good Thing: Multiple Important Group Memberships as a Source of Self-Esteem." Edited by Tom Denson. *PLOS One* 10, no. 5 (May 27, 2015): e0124609. https://doi.org/10.1371/journal.pone.0124609.

**7: In or Out**

1. Honey, Michael K. *Going Down Jericho Road: The Memphis Strike, Martin Luther King's Last Campaign*. New York: Norton, 2008.

2. J. K. Rowling, Twitter, @jk_rowling, 3:02pm, 4:09pm, 4:16pm, June 6, 2020.

3. Martin, A. E. (forthcoming). "Gender Relativism: How Context

Shapes What Is Seen as Male and Female." *Journal of Experimental Psychology: General.*

4. Anderson, Benedict. *Imagined Communities: Reflections on the Origin and Spread of Nationalism.* London and New York: Verso, 1983.

5. Seton-Watson, Hugh. *Nations and States: An Enquiry into the Origins of Nations and the Politics of Nationalism.* London: Routledge, 2020.

6. Wimmer, Andreas, and Yuval Feinstein. "The Rise of the Nation-State across the World, 1816 to 2001." *American Sociological Review* 75, no. 5 (October 2010): 764–90. https://doi.org/10.1177/0003122 410382639.

7. Hobsbawm, Eric J. *Nations and Nationalism since 1780: Programme, Myth, Reality.* Cambridge: Cambridge University Press, 1992.

8. Wilkins, Clara L., Cheryl R. Kaiser, and Heather Rieck. "Detecting Racial Identification: The Role of Phenotypic Prototypicality." *Journal of Experimental Social Psychology* 46, no. 6 (November 2010): 1029–34. https://doi.org/10.1016/j.jesp.2010.05.017.

9. Xiao, Vivian L., Brian S. Lowery, and Amelia Stillwell. "Gender Backlash and the Moderating Role of Shared Racial Group Membership." *Personality and Social Psychology Bulletin* (February 21, 2022): 014616722210745. https://doi.org/10.1177 /01461672221074543.

10. Dunbar, Adam, Charis E. Kubrin, and Nicholas Scurich. "The threatening nature of 'rap' music." *Psychology, Public Policy, and Law* 22, no. 3 (2016): 280.

11. Lips, H. M. "Women Across Cultures: Common Issues, Varied Experiences." https://www.cambridge.org/core/elements/abs/women -across-cultures/92B716F9C0DBFFA52B41056305AED048.

12. Hogg, Michael A., and Mark J. Rinella. "Social identities and shared realities." *Current Opinion in Psychology* 23 (2018): 6–10.

13. Appiah, Kwame Anthony. *Lies That Bind: Rethinking Identity.* New York: Liveright, 2019.

14. Brown, Judith K. "A Cross-Cultural Study of Female Initiation Rites." *American Anthropologist* 65, no. 4 (August 1963): 837–53. https://doi.org/10.1525/aa.1963.65.4.02a00040.

15. Docter, Richard F. *From Man to Woman: The Transgender Journey of Virginia Prince.* Northridge, CA: Docter Press, 2004.

## 8: (Re)Writing Self

1. Tsugawa, S., and H. Ohsaki. "Negative Messages Spread Rapidly and Widely on Social Media." Computer Science, Proceedings of the 2015 ACM Conference on Social Networks.

2. Cinelli, Matteo, Gianmarco De Francisci Morales, Alessandro Galeazzi, Walter Quattrociocchi, and Michele Starnini. "The echo chamber effect on social media." *Proceedings of the National Academy of Sciences* 118, no. 9 (February 23, 2021). https://www .pnas.org/doi/10.1073/pnas.2023301118.

3. Del Vicario, Michela, Alessandro Bessi, Fabiana Zollo, Fabio Petroni, Antonio Scala, Guido Caldarelli, H. Eugene Stanley, and Walter Quattrociocchi. "The Spreading of Misinformation Online." *Proceedings of the National Academy of Sciences* 113, no. 3 (January 4, 2016): 554–59. https://doi.org/10.1073/pnas.151744 1113.

4. Cinelli, Matteo, Gianmarco De Francisci Morales, Alessandro Galeazzi, Walter Quattrociocchi, and Michele Starnini. "The echo chamber effect on social media." *Proceedings of the National Academy of Sciences* 118, no. 9 (February 23, 2021). https://doi.org /10.1073/pnas.2023301118.

5. Basbanes, Nicholas A. *On Paper: The Everything of Its Two-Thousand-Year History.* New York: Vintage, 2014.

6. Rosenfeld, Michael J., Reuben J. Thomas, and Sonia Hausen. "Disintermediating Your Friends: How Online Dating in the United States Displaces Other Ways of Meeting." *Proceedings of the National Academy of Sciences* 116, no. 36 (August 20, 2019): 20190 8630. https://doi.org/10.1073/pnas.1908630116.

7. Swisher, Kara. "Serving as An Agent of Change." *Washington Post*, February 12, 1996.

8. Lloyd, Emily. "This Bridge Called My Mac: Lesbian Feminist Politics on the Internet." *Off Our Backs* 25, no. 1 (1995): 12–13.

9. Proust, Marcel. *In Search of Lost Time.* Edited by William C. Carter. Translated by C. K. Scott-Moncrieff. New Haven, CT: Yale University Press, 2013.

10. Eakin, Paul John. *Fictions in Autobiography: Studies in the Art of Self-Invention.* Princeton, NJ: Princeton University Press, 2016.

11. Kassin, Saul M., and Katherine L. Kiechel. "The Social Psychology of False Confessions: Compliance, Internalization, and Confabulation." *Psychological Science* 7, no. 3 (May 1996): 125–28. https://doi.org/10.1111/j.1467–9280.1996.tb00344.x.

12. Golding, Jonathan M., and Colin M. Macleod. *Intentional Forgetting: Interdisciplinary Approaches.* Mahwah, NJ: Erlbaum, 1998.

13. Schwartz, Barry. *The Paradox of Choice: Why More Is Less.* New York: Ecco, 2016.

14. Hunter, Dard. *Papermaking: The History and Technique of an Ancient Craft.* New York. Dover, 1978

15. Kurlansky, Mark. *Paging through History.* New York: Norton, 2016.

16. Kurlansky, Mark. *Paging through History.* New York: Norton, 2016.
17. Weber, Max, David S. Owen, and Tracy B. Strong. *The Vocation Lectures.* Indianapolis, IN: Hackett, 2004.
18. *Michael J. Bowers, Attorney General of Georgia v. Michael Hardwick, and John and Mary Doe,* 478 U.S. 186 (1986).
19. Acemoglu, Daron, and James A. Robinson. *Why Nations Fail: The Origins of Power, Prosperity and Poverty.* London: Profile Books, 2012.
20. Kessler, Friedrich. "Contracts of Adhesion—Some Thoughts about Freedom of Contract." *Columbia Law Review* 43, no. 5 (July 1943): 629. https://doi.org/10.2307/1117230.
21. Calhoun, Craig. "Nationalism and Ethnicity." *Annual Review of Sociology* 19 (August 1993): 211–39. https://doi.org/10.1146/annurev .so.19.080193.001235.
22. Sidanius, James, and Felicia Pratto. *Social Dominance: An Intergroup Theory of Social Hierarchy and Oppression.* Cambridge: Cambridge University Press, 1999.
23. Calhoun, Craig. "Nationalism and Ethnicity." *Annual Review of Sociology* 19 (August 1993): 211–39. https://doi.org/10.1146 /annurev.so.19.080193.001235.
24. Fossen, Thomas. "Political Legitimacy as an Existential Predicament." *Political Theory* (October 5, 2021): 009059172110 478. https://doi.org/10.1177/00905917211047842.
25. Lipset, Seymour Martin. "Some Social Requisites of Democracy: Economic Development and Political Legitimacy." *American Political Science Review* 53, no. 1 (1959): 69–105.
26. Tyler, Tom R. "Psychological Perspectives on Legitimacy and Legitimation." *Annual Review of Psychology* 57, no. 1 (January 2006): 375–400. https://doi.org/10.1146/annurev.psych.57.102904 .190038.
27. Devos, T., and M. R. Baanaaji. "American = White?" *Journal of Personality and Social Psychology* 88, no. 3 (2005): 447–66.
28. Mosse, George L. "Racism and Nationalism." *Nations and Nationalism* 1, no. 2 (July 1995): 163–73. https://doi.org/10.1111 /j.1354–5078.1995.00163.x.
29. Mills, Alison. "The Color of Law: A Forgotten History of How Our Government Segregated America." *Berkeley Planning Journal* 29, no. 1 (March 27, 2018). https://doi.org/10.5070/bp32913 8440.
30. Massey, Douglas S., and Nancy A. Denton. *American Apartheid: Segregation and the Making of the Underclass.* Cambridge, MA: Harvard University Press, 2003.

31. Phillips, L. Taylor, and Brian S. Lowery. "I Ain't No Fortunate One: On the Motivated Denial of Class Privilege." *Journal of Personality and Social Psychology* (June 18, 2020). https://doi.org/10.1037/pspi0000240.

32. Unzueta, Miguel M., Brian S. Lowery, and Eric D. Knowles. "How Believing in Affirmative Action Quotas Protects White Men's Self-Esteem." *Organizational Behavior and Human Decision Processes* 105, no. 1 (January 2008): 1–13. https://doi.org/10.1016/j.obhdp.2007.05.001.

## 9: What's It All For?

1. Sartre, Jean-Paul. *No Exit and Three Other Plays.* New York: Vintage Books, 1957.

2. Steger, M. F. "Experiencing meaning in life: Optimal functioning at the nexus of well-being, psychopathology, and spirituality." In P. T. P. Wong (Ed.), *The Human Quest for Meaning*, 2nd ed., pp. 165–84. New York: Routledge, 2012.

3. King, L. A., J. A. Hicks, J. Krull, and A. K. Gaiso. "Positive affect and the experience of meaning in life." *Journal of Personality and Social Psychology* 90 (2006): 179–96.

4. King, L. A. "The Commonplace Experience of Meaning in Life." *International Journal of Existential Psychology and Psychotherapy* 5, no. 1 (2014).

5. Sacks, Oliver. *The Man Who Mistook His Wife for a Hat and Other Clinical Tales.* Toronto: Knopf Canada, 2021.

6. Frankl, Viktor E. *Man's Search for Meaning.* 1946. Reprint, Boston: Beacon Press, 2006.

7. Festinger, Leon, and James M. Carlsmith. "Cognitive consequences of forced compliance." *Journal of Abnormal and Social Psychology* 58, no. 2 (1959): 203.

8. Bem, Daryl J. "Self-perception theory." In *Advances in Experimental Social Psychology*, vol. 6, pp. 1–62. San Diego, CA: Academic Press, 1972.

9. Kundera, Milan. *The Unbearable Lightness of Being.* New York: Harper & Row, 1985.

10. Nietzsche, Friedrich. *The Gay Science.* Translated by Thomas Common. Mineola, NY: Dover Philosophical Classics, 2006.

11. King, L. A. "The Commonplace Experience of Meaning in Life." *International Journal of Existential Psychology and Psychotherapy* 5, no. 1 (2014).

12. Chu, C., and B. S. Lowery. "Perceiving a Stable Self-Concept Enables the Experience of Meaning in Life."

## 10: The End?

1. Cave, Stephen. *Immortality: The Quest to Live Forever and How It Drives Civilization*. New York: Crown, 2012.
2. 2045.com. "2045 Initiative." Accessed July 6, 2022. http://2045.com/.

# Index

# About the Author

BRIAN LOWERY is the Walter Kenneth Kilpatrick Professor of Organizational Behavior at Stanford University's Graduate School of Business. Lowery's research has been published in major scholarly journals and has been covered by media outlets such as the *Washington Post*, GQ, *Psychology Today*, *Pacific Standard*, *Quartz*, *Huffington Post*, and NPR's *All Things Considered*. He also hosts the podcast *Know What You See*.